# WORLD WAR 3

## AN IMAGINARY AND TOTAL DISASTER

HIMANK MITTAL

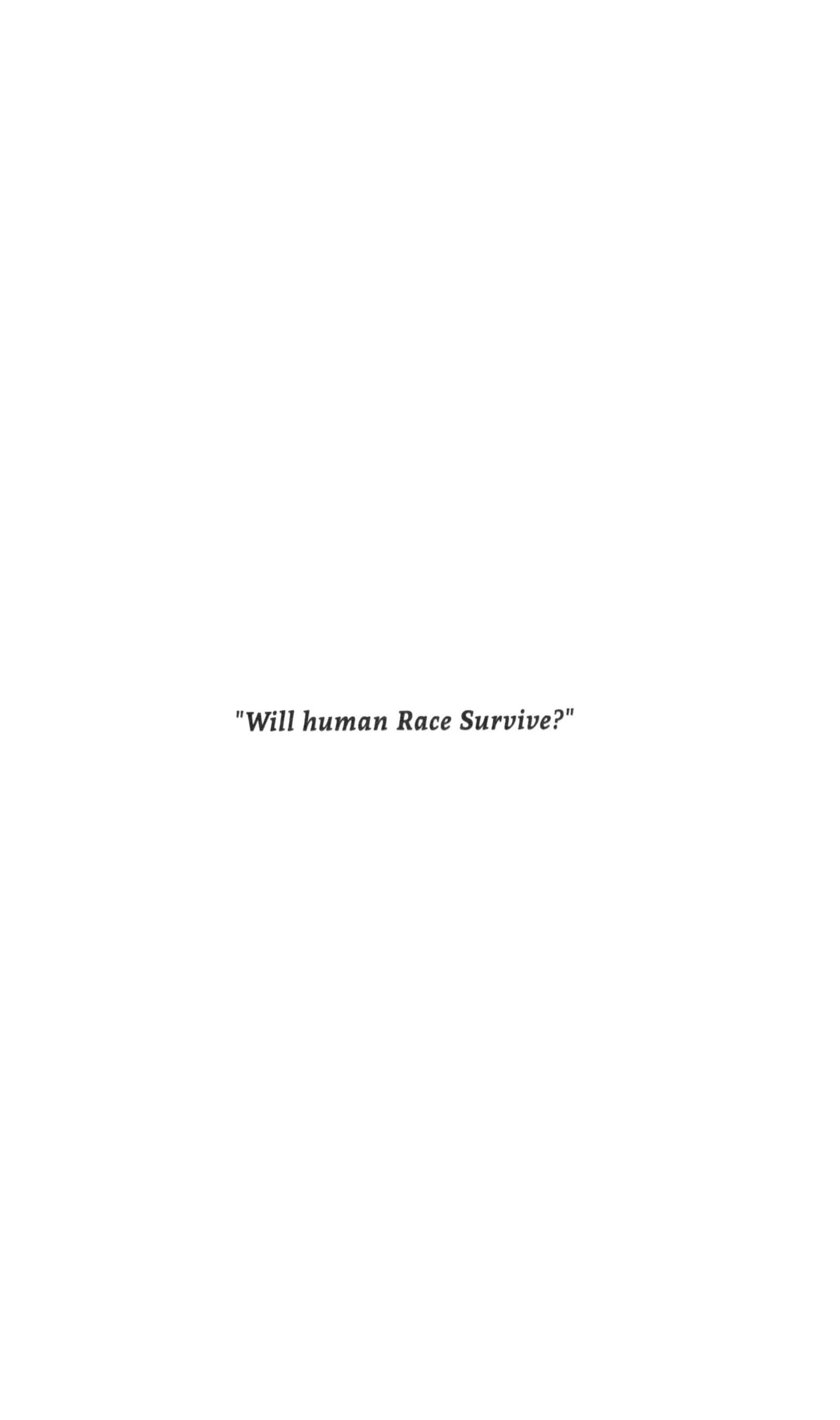

"Will human Race Survive?"

# Contents

# About The Author

As the author of this book, I, Himank Mittal, enjoy acquiring knowledge through the internet and have a keen interest in various subjects, including airplanes and geopolitics. My hobbies include playing the guitar, drawing, and solving Rubik's cubes. I reside in Gurugram, Vatika Sector-82, and have written two books: Politics of the World and Airplanes Part 1. I have a strong affinity for technology, and my writing is published through Notion Press. Thank you very much for your purchase.

# Preface

"I do not know with what weapons World War III will be fought, but World War IV will be fought with sticks and stones." – Albert Einstein. This profound insight from one of the greatest minds of our time underscores the devastating impact that a potential World War III could have on our world. As Einstein also poignantly stated, "Wars do not have honor, only death."

This book, as suggested by its title, delves into the concept of a hypothetical World War III. It is important to state that we stand firmly against the occurrence of such a catastrophic event, and we hope you share this sentiment. The content within may not align with everyone's interests or perspectives, so please approach it with an open mind and do not take any part of it too seriously.

Our exploration includes possible scenarios that could unfold in a World War III, including potential fronts and strategies that nations might employ. We also consider the role of nuclear weapons, though we aim to maintain a level of realism by not exaggerating their usage. Additionally, we will discuss the stance of neutral countries and delve into related conflicts such as the Cold War.

I extend my gratitude to Adobe Stock, Alarmy and other map providers for providing the images used in this book. It is important to emphasize that this book is not intended to offend or predict any real-world events. The content is based on my current worldview and publicly available military information.

For any inquiries, please contact: nitinmittal316@gmail.com.

# ONE
## HISTORY OF THE CONFLICT

**World War three- From where did this term arrive?**

World war three term has no original dateline from where it originated. But a trace of some events might define a basic outline of where it originated. Now, to know what could happen if such war erupts, we need to know its origin. Thanks to the internet available and the great researchers of the world, we got a trace of it.

After World War 1 and 2 no one wanted such a devastating loss of life, property and mostly civilizations. But, the big superpowers, That were and are known as the United States of America and The Union of Soviet Socialists Republics wanted to have a strong hold over the world and a new competition raised, today known as the cold war. But they were not fighting, this war was about who influences the world, they compete in almost every field, even if it was space or earth. They showed nations that they are the best and small nations had no choice but to choose between them. Many groups were made to stop this cold war, and some of them lasted for long too. But in last, almost every small nation got stuck in a war and needed support and finally joined a team. They fought for power and from there a new term arrived, World War three.

These countries could fight anytime and could destroy the world. Many incidents happened when in a war both were in different teams, but they never fought to each other. sometimes they were about to directly war with each other. One example was the Cuban missile crisis when United states of America tried to attack Cuba but Cuba knew it and asked help From Union of Soviet Socialists Republics and in retaliation, they send nuclear weapons in Cuba to help them! Later on, United states of America signed a deal in which there was that United States would not attack Cuba but USSR will have to take back their nukes from Cuba. Both agreed. But, Because of many small mistakes made by the USSR government a little spark finally led to the desolation of it into independent countries. United States took all nukes of A new formed country from the dissolved USSR known as Ukraine. Russia was a little stronger so didn't give up nukes. But the World War three concept was now of no meaning. The competition was finished and Russia was not enough strong to fight a global war. Other countries weren't very strong and so there is no risk of any other global concept. The world had now bigger problems like economic crisis's, oil prices at hike, establishing relations with the new formed countries and all.

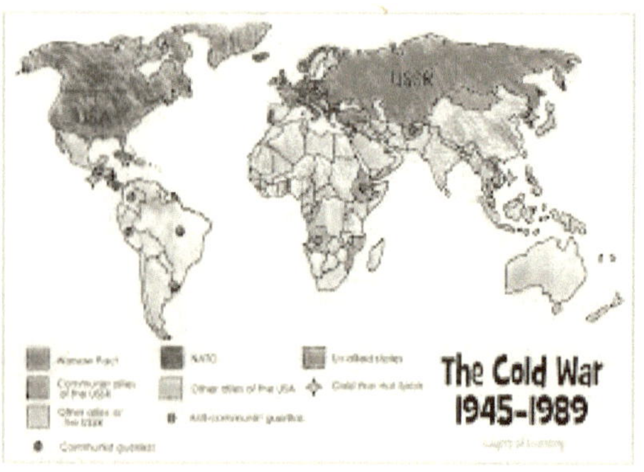


Cold war

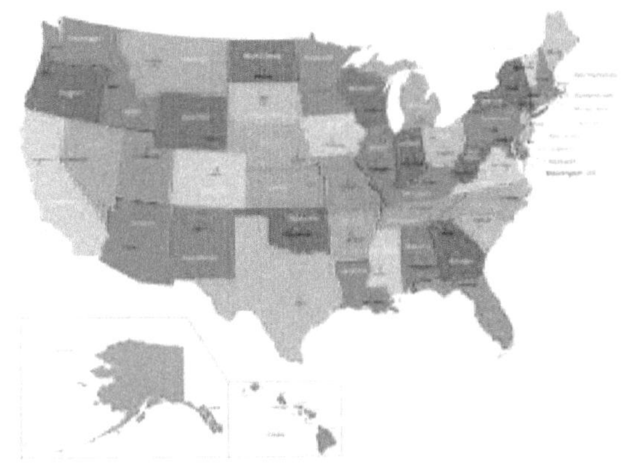

United states- States map

Dissolved Soviet Union

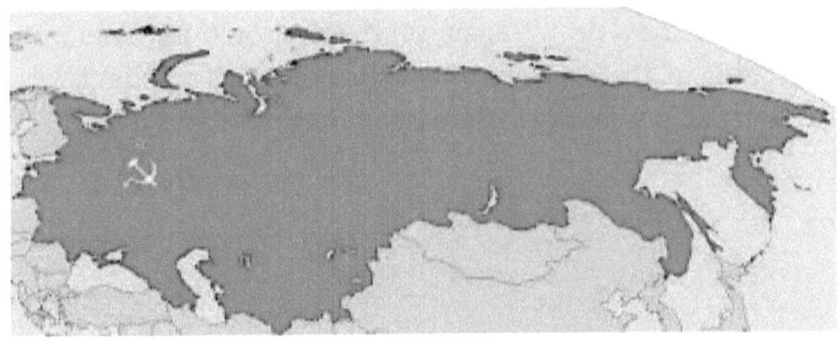

Soviet Union

## Revival of this conflict

But how did this topic revive again? Well, countries started to develop, and more developed nations arrived with new ideologies and ideas. One of the fastest growing was a big country with large population and strong military-China. Russia also started to recover and China was also followed the USSR ideology started to influence soviet friendly countries that had no option. Weak countries who support USSR previously wanted a new country for them and China took the opportunity.

Although, Russia also emerged but China was much stronger and Russia was weaker and, on the flipside, China had a large and cheap labor force so more and more companies shifted their manufacturing there. China's economy boomed and China spent more and more money to influence the world. United States did not like the idea of a new competition who was not of their ideology. China was an aggressive country and tried to attack its neighbors like Taiwan, South Korea and Japan and United States had relationship with these countries so it started to militarize these countries heavily and China also retaliated by the same action but on the flipside.

On the other hand, developing counties like India, Pakistan, Israel, Palestine, Ukraine and Russia had conflicts and started conflicts again all over the world. As there were no two mainstream sides countries had no/ less fear of losing. Now, this conflict started to rise again and took some years to evolve and now people again got the view of World War 3. So, in this book we're going to discuss about this topic only. This conflict is huge and I will try to cover all possibilities. Here is an image of about this.

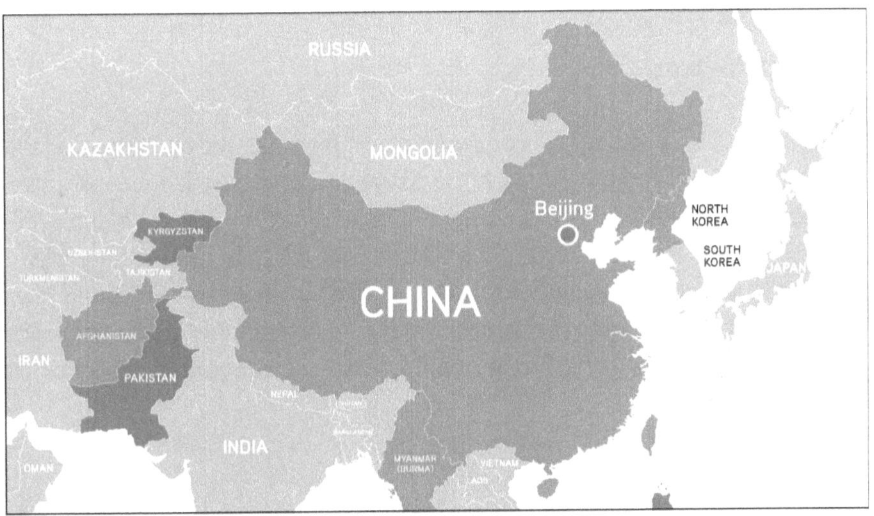


China

Red countries are countries who are dependent of China for their existence and are allies of China. Dark grey countries are countries that are allies of China but are not as dependent on China. This shows that China is very powerful. There are thousands of images like this on the internet and so check it out.

## Neutral Countries

To fully grasp this topic, it's important to identify the countries that maintain a truly neutral stance and are likely to avoid engaging in war. Notable examples include Switzerland, Iceland, Austria, Malta, Luxembourg, and Liechtenstein, all of which have maintained neutrality for many years, with policies that emphasize non-involvement and minimal war experience. These nations will likely steer clear of conflict.

Additionally, Africa and South America are expected to remain largely unaffected or untouched by the war, as they have little vested interest in the conflict. While Africa could potentially be drawn into the war, South America is most likely to stay uninvolved. Keeping these factors in mind, we will explore the possible Fronts that could emerge in this global confrontation.

## Nuclear Aspect

In this book, to add a layer of realism and intrigue, we will consider the use of nuclear weapons. However, the usage will be limited—not excessive, but also not absent. Specifically, only 15 nuclear warheads will be deployed, given that 13 countries possess them. Some nations may launch one or two additional strikes, bringing the total to 15. This limited use of nukes allows the world to avoid complete destruction, leaving room for a potential peace treaty. This aspect will be further explored in the micro-topics section of Chapter 7. Thank you!

# TWO
## SCENARIOS BASICS

*So these are going to be the fronts we're going to discuss:-*

- 1$^{st}$: Korean front
- 2$^{nd}$: Russian fronts
- 3$^{rd}$: India-Pakistan-China front
- 4$^{th}$: Middle eastern front
- 5$^{th}$: Caucasian front
- 6$^{th}$: Taiwanese front

**FRONTS:**

*Korean front:*

So as the name suggests the Korean peninsula could go to war. There are two countries in the Korean peninsula namely South Korea and North Korea which have disputes for years and are very hostile to each other. The Korean border is one of the most militarized borders in the world. But only these two countries would not go to war some more countries would get involved like China, Japan and USA. This would be a whole massacre. South Korea is the 6$^{th}$ strongest country in the world and North Korea is the 34rth. But north Korea has an advantage of Nukes as they have nukes and South Korea hasn't. China will go with North Korea and South Korea will get support from USA and Japan. These both countries went into a war in 1954 which took lives of millions of people. It was known as the Korean war. It also went something like that similarly with only some differences. South Korea will most probably win but wars cannot be predicted so anything could happen. Also, this war could also spark a World War three because demilitarized zone has many tourists and South Korea also has many tourists so if a war is sparked these tourists could die and could make other countries join.

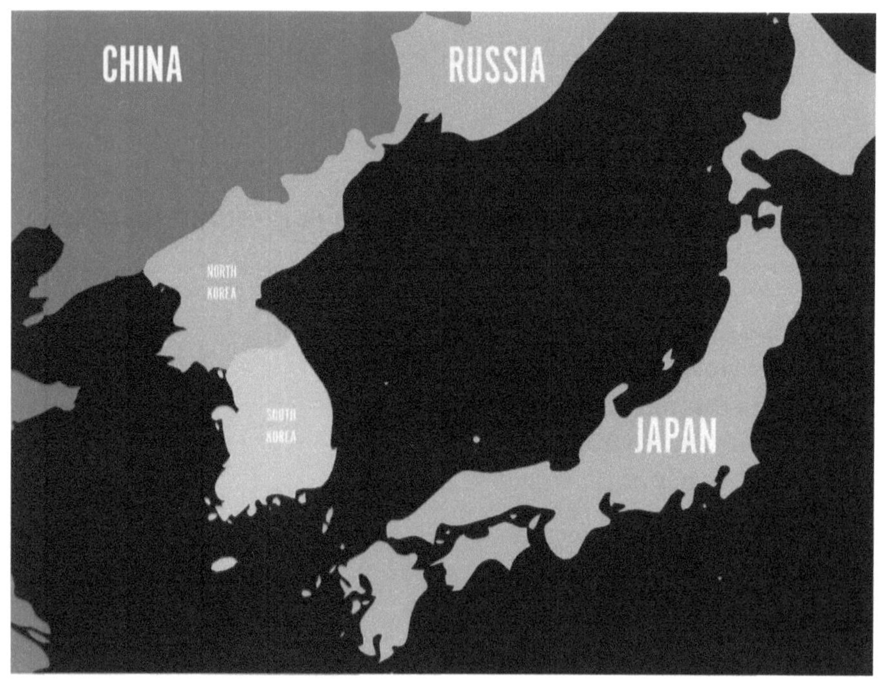


The Korean Front

## *Russian Front:*

So, this war in going to be in Europe. This war could spark between NATO and Russia. Russia and NATO have been enemies for years and NATO's main goal is to stop expansion of Russia into Europe. For the past few years Russia has been aggressive on NATO's borders and put-up nukes near them. Meanwhile NATO has expanded their borders and militarized them heavily, and this war is going to be huge as Russia is the world's 2 strongest power and 1$^{st}$ in landmass.

But NATO is also not weak as it has world's strongest superpower United States and many more powerful countries. If we plus both sides nuke the numbers of nukes both have is almost the same. NATO has allies in the pacific like Japan and South Korea while Russia has allies like China, Pakistan and North Korea. Both sides almost have similar strength so it will be interesting who would win. NATO has an advantage of world dominance and Regular military practices. Russia's strongest ally is China and NATO's is Japan. But we should not forget that NATO is a defensive alliance of countries and so NATO gets an extra advantage of a lot of ideas of invasion and strong countries like United States, United Kingdom, France, Germany and Poland which have strong militaries and could attack Russia badly.

This war would be bad for Russia as the Russia's economy would crash that we are seeing in the Russia - Ukraine war that the western sanctions destroyed Russia. Europe is dependent on Russia for its oil but if they are on a war, they would have to use far Alternatives like Saudi Arabia and Iran and not to mention they are Russia's Allies.

## *INDIA- PAKISTAN-CHINA FRONT:*

You know how big of this controversy is, every one fighting over an area of Kashmir, and if you don't know why these countries fight for it, first of all the region has natural resources that are very rare and second of all the area is filled with beautiful hills and mountains. When India- Pakistan Partition was made Kashmir was an Independent country but Pakistan attacked Kashmir and the king of the region asked help from India and India helped them but they signed a deal that Kashmir will be an Indian State and so this deal was signed now Pakistani soldiers captured half of Kashmir and because of the mountains there India found it hard to push them back all over so they pushed them a little back and signed a deal which gave some part of Kashmir to India and some to Pakistan and Till now they both are fighting to capture the whole area and have fought many wars. But then, how did China enter this conflict? Well Pakistan didn't had money so they sold some part of Kashmir to them and China invaded India in 1962 and India lost it because India was not prepared so China took Aksai Chin a part from Kashmir and Claims Arunachal Pradesh from India till now.

Aside from this if we see the military strength of these countries Pakistan is at number 9 and China is at no 3 and India is at no 4. China and Pakistan are allies. But India and China don't have a long border as most of it is covered by the tallest mountain range The Himalayas. Indian Army has a good experience in mountain ranges so they would win is such a war against China. India has a very strong hand over Pakistan especially in wars. The war of Indo- Pak of 1965, Bangladesh liberation of 1971, Kargil war of 1999. Even the big superpowers Like USA and NATO are with India. Also, China has to fight in many fronts like Russian front and Korean front with superpowers so if India wins it wouldn't be a surprise. India has strategies of fighting two nations together for years so that they could win. Also, these three of them are nuclear powers so a nuclear war could be possible.

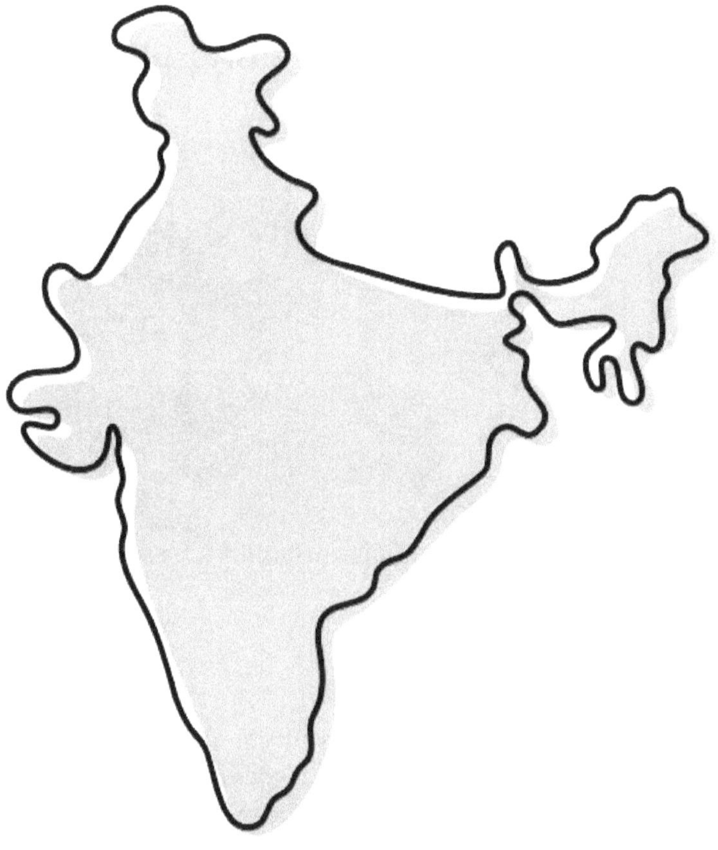

INDIA

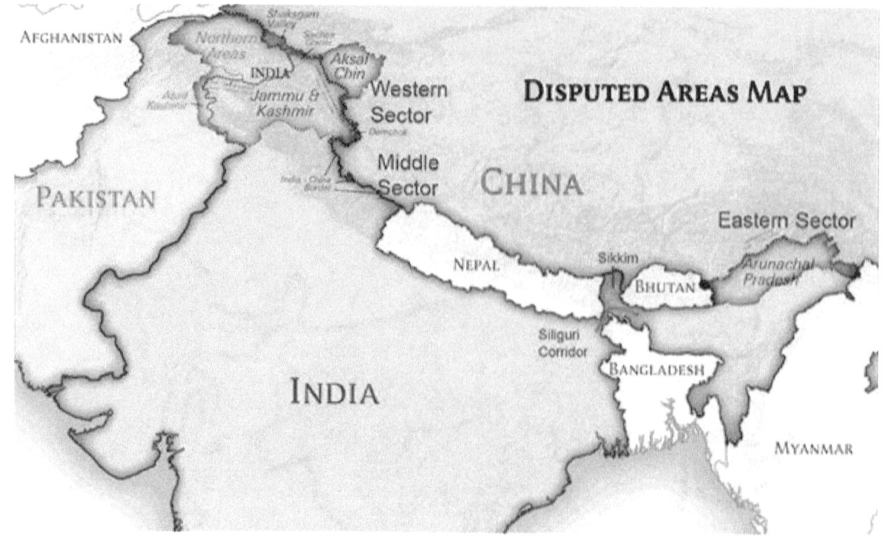


India-Pakistan-China dispusted Area map

## *Middle-Eastern Front:*

Middle east on its own is a very complex subcontinent present on the Asia continent and has many Muslims. But countries hate each other a lot. Iran and Saudi Arabia and Israel Palestine are the predominant conflicts in the continent. Syrian civil war is destroying the country and Turkey is taking the advantage by invading them very secretly. Although the civil war is slowing down and coming to an end it is still taking a lot of life's and is a house for terrorists who kill civilians who even haven't done anything and not only in Syria but all over the world. Only Israel has nukes in Middle east and Israel takes a lot of advantage of this.

Israel also has the **WORLD'S BEST SECRET AGENCIES** LIKE Mossad and more. Middle east is full of terrorists and Most countries on the subcontinent hate Israel but United States support Israel and Israel Palestine conflict started when Israel was partitioned by the United Nations. When The State of Israel was declared Palestine along with their Muslim friends attacked Israel and the newly created state of Israel made Many countries loose in only 6 days! From then on, Middle east hates Israel a lot. But Israel will never lose it seems. Iran is trying to make nuclear weapons secretly but United States find it and destroys their plans. Although Iran could not do anything against Israel, they established A new terrorist organization that is very strong and does wars against Israel Frequently and is known as Hezbollah. Palestine has been carved up by Israel in years and Palestine in Run by two agencies, A terrorist organization The government of Palestine controlling the West bank of Palestine and Hamas that took control of the Gaza strip in Palestine and now controls it. Gaza strip is like a prison because of no food, water cannot be imported as it is surrounded by Israel.

Hamas is also a terrorist organization. But Hamas has made an network of tunnels that they use to transport goods from all over the world and Israel is not able to find it for years. Saudi Arabia and Iran are enemies as they both are Muslim countries but both countries have different types of Muslims and fight for world domination. A bad war could erupt in this area and would crash world economy as the area is filled with oil and most of the world's oil is exported from these countries only. There would be oil crisis and also interestingly stop the wars in the world because of no oil and this would be a surprising ending.

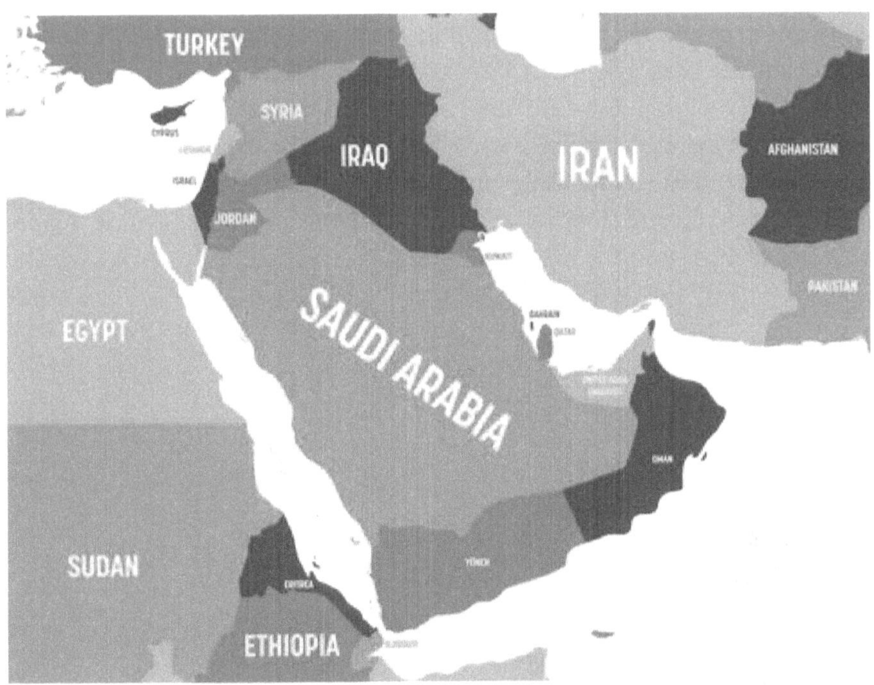

Middle eastern Front

## *Caucasian front:*

Georgian front is a very dedicated front as Russia is also a very aggressive country towards Georgia, they have attacked Georgia and captured some area but no one recognizes it that's something else. Georgia is a small country and could be defeated by Russia easily. Georgia not very strong in any of the world's rankings that could hold them but USA will not allow Russia to capture Georgia and help them a lot in case of war like currently in Russia Ukraine war USA helped Ukrainians and that is why Ukraine is still able to fight a war with double their strength. We have to admit that Russia has a very old supply of weapons and they will easily lose any war in case of fought with an US ally or USA itself as they have very old weapons and they cannot use their Nukes because Georgia is a small country and if a nuke is fired Russia would also have to face the nuclear dust from it. But now let's talk about the Asian front that is between two neighboring countries Armenia and Azerbaijan. This is not related to Russia. Russia supports Armenia but wouldn't be able to do so because of many fronts to fight. Armenia has Allies like USA and EU and Azerbaijan has allies like Turkey and Pakistan. For reference turkey is the 11th strongest country in the world and Pakistan is the ninth and US and EU I already told you. Both Sides have Nukes but Armenia's Allies have more. This war will most probably be won by Armenia and Georgia war will be probably won by Georgia. Again, this war will be close.

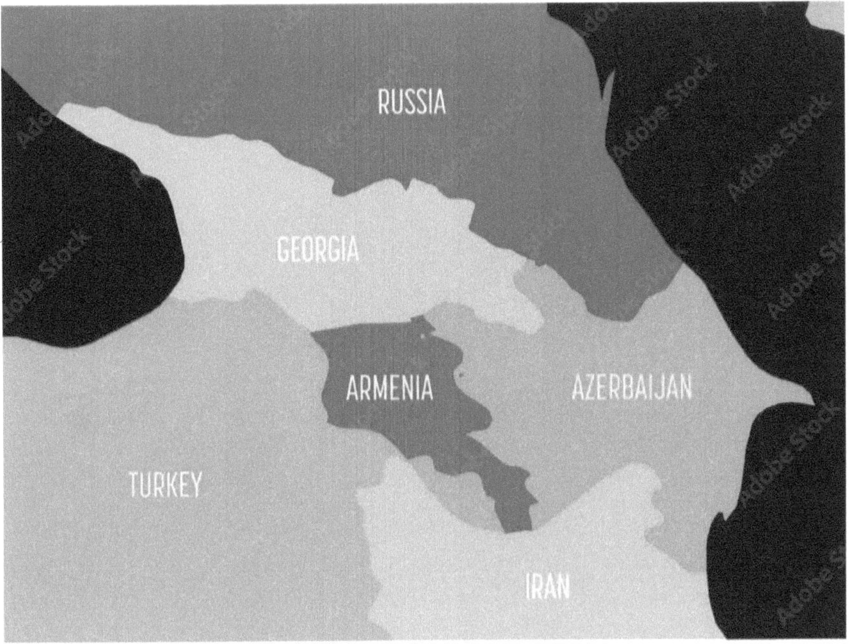



Caucasian Front

## *Taiwanese Front:*

This, according to me is the Easiest Front I could explain. Taiwan- China! Everyone knows this. So, I am going to explain this in short. China is a super powerful country- and a country which is equally running against the United States. But to explain this conflict we have to go in History. So, after World War 2 The Chinese liberation party was thrown out of the mainland China and was left on the Island of Taiwan. China's people republic of China party captured the mainland, China. Now Mainland China is mostly known as China today and the Island is known as Taiwan. Now China doesn't recognize Taiwan and Taiwan doesn't recognize China. Both Claim them to be real China and Has led to many conflicts. China as a big power doesn't want any US ally around their country and China wants the extra advantage of the sea access of Taiwan. Also, we cannot forget the small country/nation of Hongkong. Hongkong is a not as valuable as Taiwan so but China doesn't want any neighbors and wants to rule the world so they consider Hongkong as a nation inside their country. So, these are all about fronts!

China- Taiwan Front

Now, lets look about the

## TOP TEN powers of the world:

### *(According to 2024- from Firepower Index)*

1. USA
2. Russia
3. China
4. India
5. South Korea
6. United Kingdom
7. Japan

8. Turkey
9. Pakistan
10. Italy

**Choke Points:-**

**These are the choke points that could disturb supplies:-**

1. *Malacca strait*

2. *Arabic Sea*

3. *Suez Canal*

4. *Panama Canal*

5. *Gibraltar Point*

6. *Black Sea*

### *Short Summary of all-*

### *1. Malacca Strait*

**Malacca Strait** is a point around Indonesia which contributes to 70% of goods transportation of China which is again to summaries the world's Factory. Every Big company **has mostly** manufactured in China. World economy would shake and crumble and most probably be in another rescission like 2008 and even bad then that if it is blocked. It would be the most devastating crisis of the world. And we could not forget that Semiconductor producing Taiwan also is very important for the world because for those who don't know what semiconductor is, it is a small computer that is the brain of our electronic devices (Mostly except some) and very important countries like Japan and South Korea would also be crumbled because fighting China without the help of USA will be hard. But the Twist is that the planning of blocking this was made By USA only. Although USA being thousands of Kilometers far away from its USA was planning with India which has Andaman and Nicobar Islands that are very near to Malacca Strait to block Malacca strait for China if USA's any Ally gets attacked by China. The strategy is excellent but super difficult. India if they do this will have to put their Navy in Indian Ocean and it is so big. We have an argue that Indian Navy is very big and I agree with that but if India does its India to execute successfully will have to use their 1/4rth navy that on its own is a very big number considering as Navy in a situation of War has to Defend the country, Block other country and Attack other country's navy and another task will be hard to manage considering if they do so China a big power will attack India so this will be a very difficult task for India.

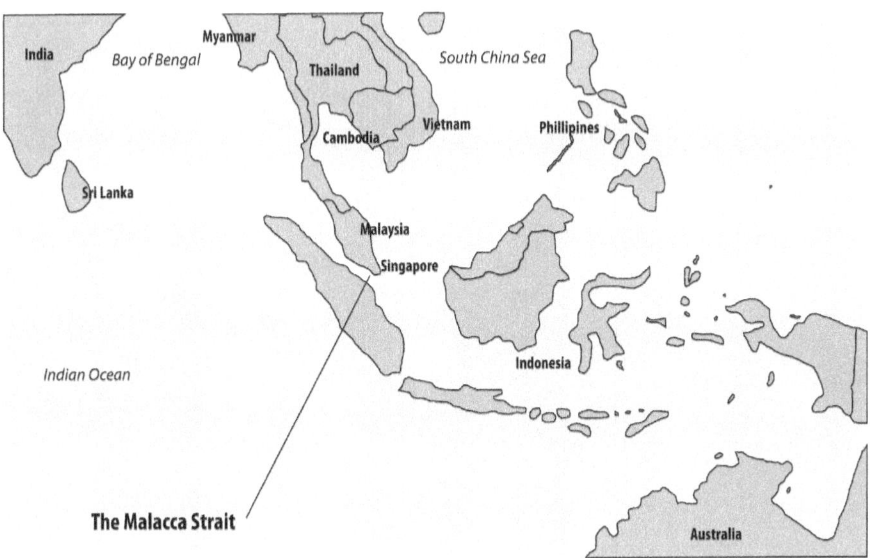


Malacca Strait

## *2. Arabic Sea (Gulf of Oman)*

**Arabic Sea** has one of the biggest boundaries with the oil rich countries. All mostly Arab countries are oil rich and their oil is exported by a path and the starting part of the route is Arabic Sea. To be specific the oil rich countries I am considering are United Arab Emirates (UAE) which some people know as Abu Dhabi or Dubai, Saudi Arabia, Iran, Qatar, and Bahrain. Also, this Choke point could stop the war! Interesting but how? If the oil supplies are cut countries will not be able to get oil to fight the war and there would be oil shortage. Although this is not very much possible but maybe some areas it could pause war. We cannot forget that they're other countries too those who have oil. But this would make war one sided because those countries are mostly Russia and China's friend and Russia on its own is a very oil rich country. But let's not get into opinions and let's be only on facts. But this could lead to a Middle- eastern war which as we saw in the history always are very bloody so we should avoid any power blocking point of **Gulf of Oman.**

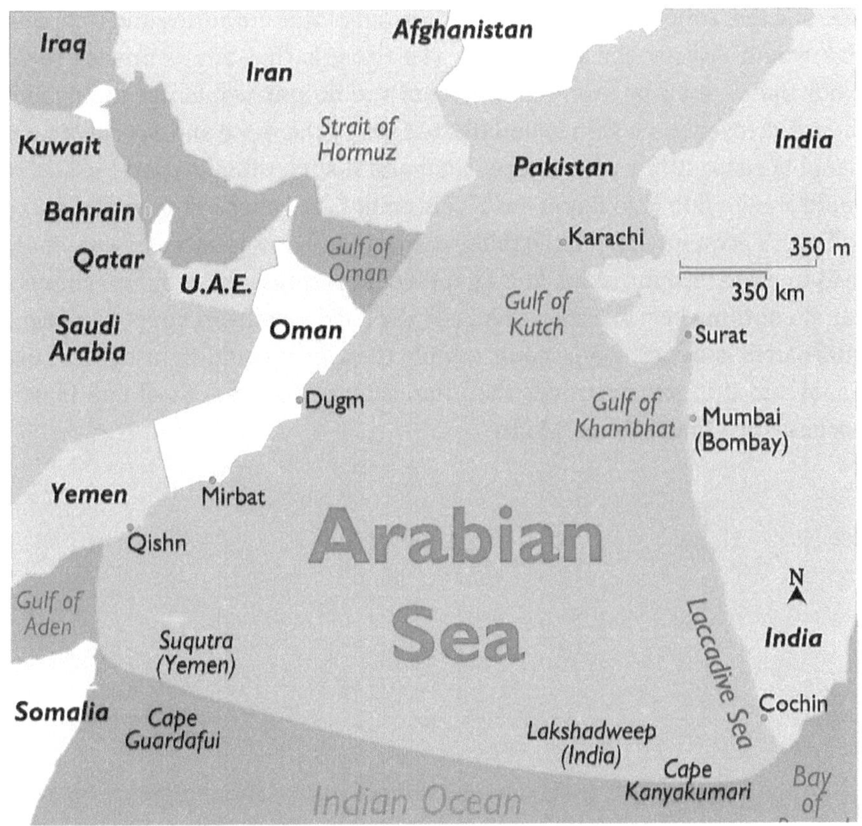


Gulf of Oman blokage can lead to war

## 3. SUEZ CANAL:

**Suez Canal** is one of the most important routes for the world. Although it may seem not very important but it is. World's 30% trade goes through it. It connects trade from Asia to Europe and vice versa and the Indian Ocean bordering countries and Oceania. Plus, this can be done by Somalian expert pirates who hijack ships and Yemenite recently rising Yehudi Rebels and the constructor and Owner of this canal Egypt too. This would again shake the world economy as we saw a few months back when a ship was stuck in the canal and in days world had to bear hundreds of millions, billions and crores losses of goods. This could shake the world because if any country bombs this Canal the world who needs exports and imports to even run a war and fast transfer of soldiers to Allies and of Ammunitions and weapons, this would destroy the whole war. The thing is that any countries could block these canals by just bombing them and no ship would like their goods to be destroyed so no ship would like to pass by the route and Specially Suez Canal becuase it is a man- made canal and if something is destroyed there could lead to floods in Egypt but if this point is not chocked then could lead to Egypt's economy to boom during war time as every country in war would lead to more weapon ships and Egypt would increase price but no country can do nothing becuase they also need the good help from Egypt as a faster alternative is better. Egypt could supply the war it could fight by the Suez Canal and if it gets destroyed then the Sea will get more Steel and Plastic becuase the Canal is Man- Made.

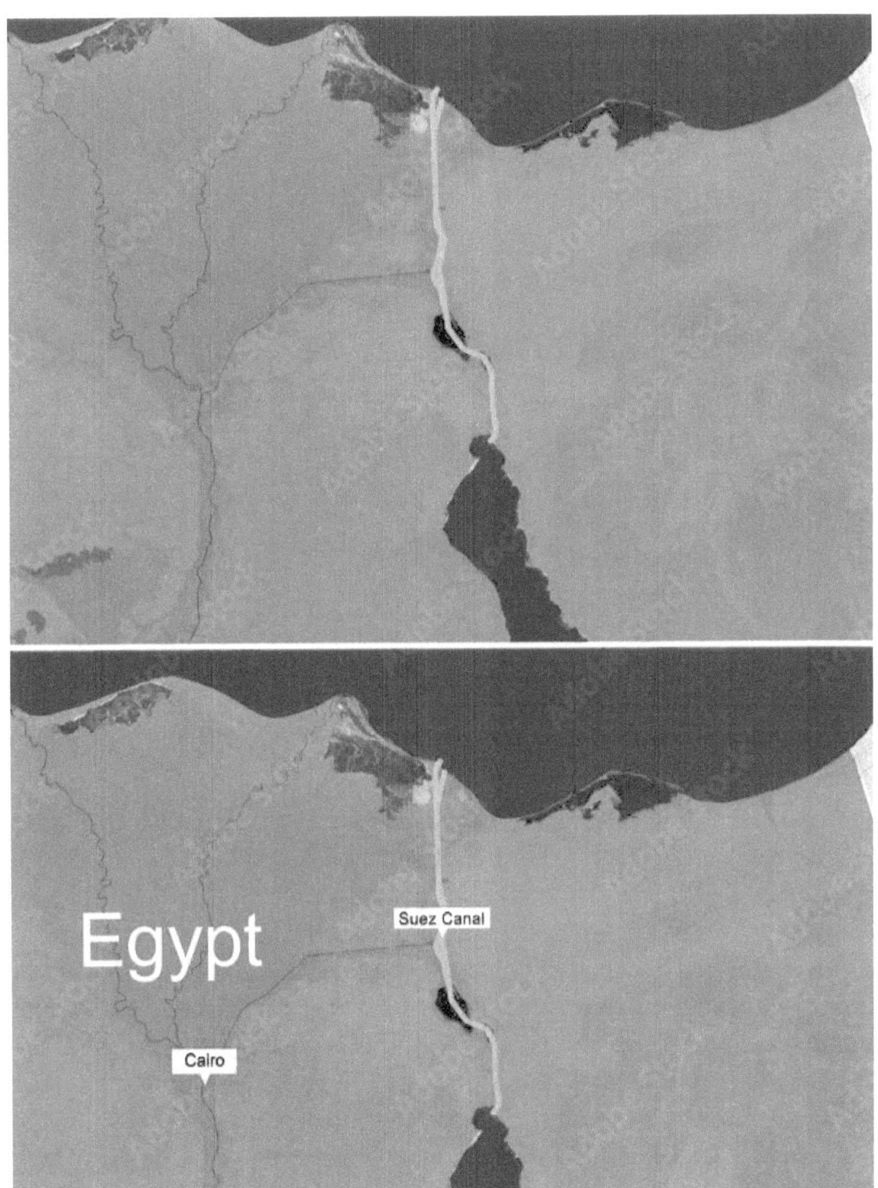


Self explaining

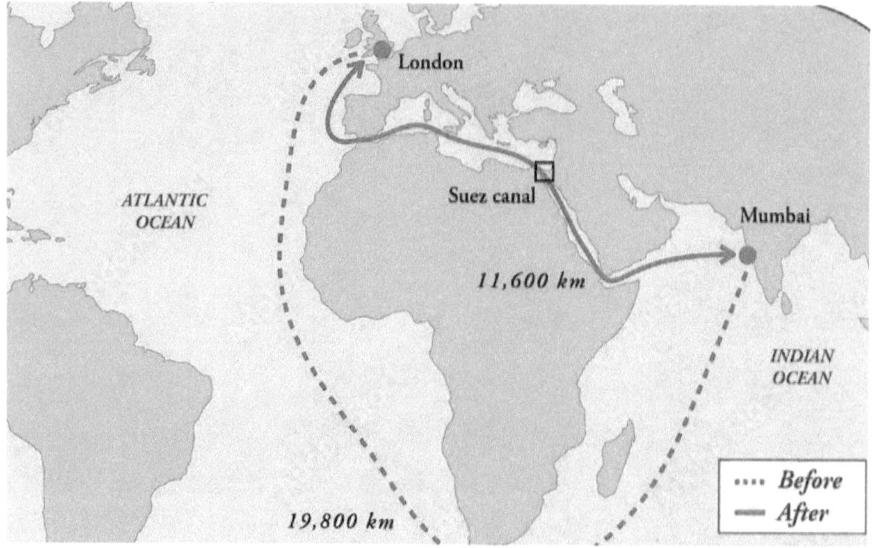



Explaning the short route of Suez Canal

# 4. Panama Canal

**Panama Canal** is also a man- Made Canal that is a shortcut so that good don't have to pass through both continents of North America and South America and can pass through a cut between both. If it is bombed then would mostly destroy the Eco- System of Panama. The control of this Canal would be with United States but this Canal wouldn't effect the world economy much compared to the other points we have discussed and would not create an economic crisis. Although this is controlled by Panama but Panama doesn't have an sizeable Army so United States provides military assistance to Panama. But if it is destroyed United States highly economicly active area's Importing and Exporting to Europe would be cut and they would have to move goods to the other side of the country and then take a big route and this would take alot of time. As I have said many times that speed matters in war situation. United States have to supply Europe during war to help them. China could also capture the canal to its use. They have some allies around it.

Panama Canal

## 5. Gibraltar Point

**Gibraltar Point** on the Spanish peninsula but is controlled by the British and is the starting point for Mediterranean Sea. It has Spain on one side and Morocco on the other Side. This point is important route of Transportation for countries who only have access to the Mediterranean Sea or only have the access to the black Sea to Import and Export Goods to the America's. Although they have a route through Suez Canal the route itself is very huge. Also, America has played a huge role in Europe so they also have to travel that way. Although this route cannot be bombed becuase it will have no effect becuase it is so deep and the only way to block it is by Ships that could be destroyed so there is no such worry of **permanent** blockage but will temporarily create huge waves towards the neighboring countries that could lead to Tsunamis. but this gap is not very big that it can't be filled with multiple ships so Russia to its advantage block this strait before United States comes to help Europe. But it could block some important powers like Israel, turkey, Italy, Debatably Ukraine and Partially Russia because Russia mostly has the option of using of this route only becuase the other route is mostly controlled by its opponents but this route has less USA allies from Americas. The Suez Canal route is also Interlinked with it and if both are blocked the Mediterranean Sea bordering countries will be blocked from rest of the world. But there is more contrast to it as we talk about the next Choke point.

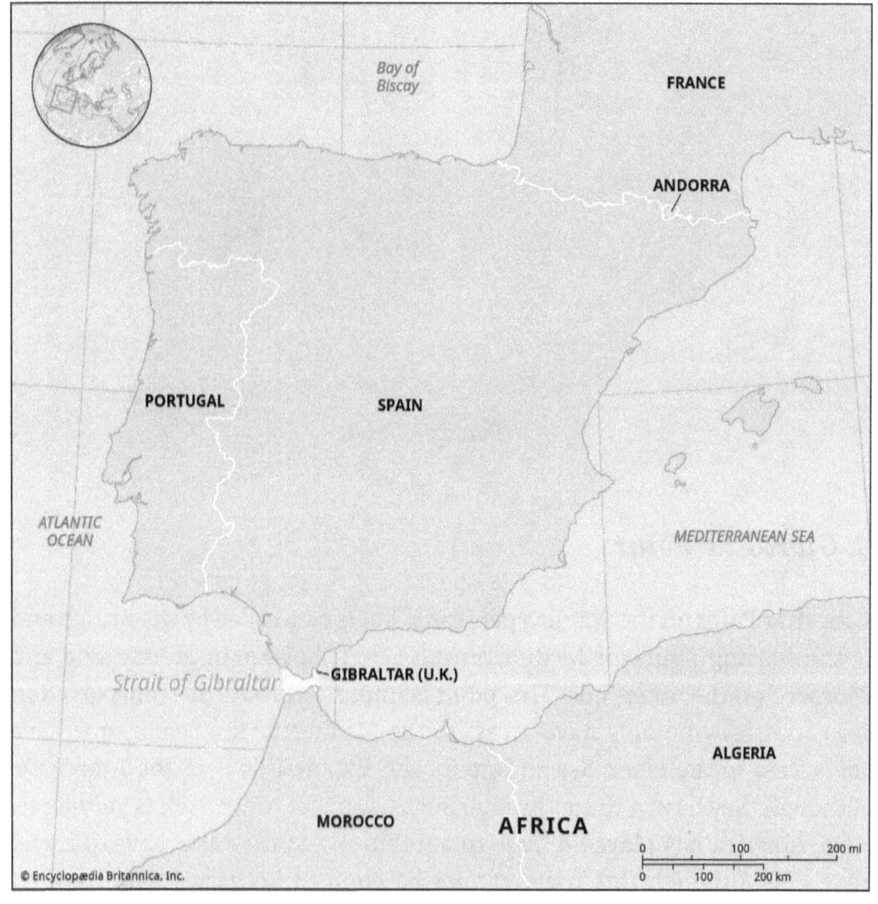


Strait of Gibratar

## 6. Black Sea

**Black SEA** is not very big topic to discuss but it plays a role in the chocking points. If Suez Canal, Gibraltar point, and Black Sea is blocked Then Italy, Algeria, Tunisia, Libya, Israel, Syria, Lebanon, Turkey, Greece, Romania, Bulgaria, Ukraine's coastlines will be useless and will be disconnected from the rest of the world. The Black Sea entry is controlled by Turkey. Funn fact is that the line of division between Asia and Europe also passes through the black Sea entry. There are not many important countries for the world except Ukraine and Russia. The entry to the Black Sea is known as Bosporus. Now this is for this Chapter.

Black Sea

# THREE

## DESTRUCTION, STRATEGIES & MORE

**DESTRUCTION:**

This war is going to be for sure between Russia- EU- USA- China- India will alone shake the world economy and About 1/3 of the world will be at war.

But now think that the countries of Koreas, Japan, Taiwan join the war and now the whole semiconductor world is at war. Now the whole world will not have any semiconductors and that means no satellites, Phones, Laptops, washing machines and all electronics gone.

Now think that Pakistan, Iran, Israel, UK, NATO, Ukraine joins the war. Now the whole world economy will be destroyed. But let's add the last addition that Brazil, Argentina, Venezuela, Mexico, Canada and Colombia join the war. Now you can safely say that the world economy is in total recession and this is the real smaller image of the World War 3.

2/3 of the world will be at the war this time. World will be in ashes and most of the countries equipped with nuclear power have been included in this war. Also, there will be more changes between the diplomacy of countries as almost half of the world have elections this year in 2024.

# STRATEGIES:

***only of the top 4 most powerful countries***
**sorry other readers we'll make a separate book for you too!**
**I must have made for top 3 only but top 4 considers more population and I want more people to know about thier country.**

## *United States of America:*

So United States of America most probably when Russia uses nukes on Europe USA will fire nukes on the nuclear launching centers of Russia so that Russia doesn't get to attack United States of America and then when they are safe, they will retaliate with nukes to Russia and will attack on their military bases and major cities and finish their whole power. For China, USA will also try the strategy but USA doesn't know much about China's Main bases so they will avoid doing so and maybe be destroyed and they will try to attack on Chinese trade centers and will block Malacca Strait for China so that their economy shatters. Also, they would try to destroy their ports so that China's weak allies have no other option but to ally to USA or the west. Also, USA's big navy power will block all the weak allies of China with their navy and Airforce and force them to join them or get destroyed. United States Navy is already all around the world and will easily Defeat weak nations. United States only has one strategy for North Korea that nukes their Nukes or they will get a nuclear rainfall of 40 nukes. But North Korea is very Isolated and only their supreme leader Kim Jong Un only knows that where the nukes are situated and even the nuke makers don't know where they are. The people who placed them are killed instantly after they have placed them so that no one knows anything about them. Apart from Kim Jong Un only one person that is his kid only knows where the nukes are. Even the top officials of the country don't know.

## *RUSSIAN FEDERATION:*

Russian Federation has the Hitler strategy, Instant kill. They had the plan to destroy the whole Ukraine in 5 days! But that didn't happen and becuase of the long time of war Russia is in Rescission. Now Russia's this war has proven than that Russia as a 3 strongest country cannot win a war with their Strategy especially if it is west's Allies. Although it was a good strategy for small countries but not with big countries. Although this isn't Russia's only strategy, they also have a defense strategy that as soon as the invaders come in, they will bomb all their houses even the Russian People and Run away back and will repeat this process until the invaders are not let with any supplies or are killed becuase of the cold conditions or the ammunitions are finished. Russia is so big that Invading it Fully is not possible so the invading force after a lot of travelling gives up and this strategy has also helped Russia win many wars. Although we don't currently know that Russian people do still have the will to destroy their houses and will the leader Vladimir Putin want to destroy all the infrastructure just to win a war. But if they do they will win a war and their economy will be shattered and they will be a land of destroyed buildings. But surely if they do so and win the war, they will take a lot of money to agree to peace so that they could rebuild their country and still the money is not sure to be enough to repair the country and the country would starve to hunger and water and most importantly another country could attack them and Russian people who would be rebuilding their houses would give up.

**Current Strategy:** Russia knows it cannot defeat USA in normal warfare. So, it is defeating USA in the other war, the network war. Despite Russia being in a war with Ukraine, Russia president Putin is on a world tour, first went to N. Korea, then to Vietnam, met Xi Xing Ping and Narendera Modi met him in person in Russia itself. Plus, In October Russia has gotten the golden opportunity to host the BRICKS+ summit. Russia has formed a team with North Korea and north Korean troops are invited on the frontline of Ukraine to fight the war. They have started De- Dollarization and China is helping them. With their growing reach to the world, De- Dollarization will be increased and after many years USA's first pillar will fall, Dollar. Then Russia can target the other two pillars, Military force (the hardest) and the ally network of USA and these three pillars are helping the USA stand as the world's superpower and if anyone has destroyed these pillars USA will fall as a superpower and a new world order will be established.

**Mission Impossible:** This mission is launched just a few months before. This includes destruction of nuclear arsenals. Not of Russia, but of all nuclear armed nations of Europe so that Europe doesn't have power to do any nuclear launches against Russia and by that Russia will not be harmed on a large scale which can help them which against NATO. Here's how it will work:-

**Defensive part:** Under this mission Russia will on its defensive part will make thousands and lakhs of nuclear bunkers for its public and safeguard them.

**Offensive part:** Under the offensive part, means the main mission, they will reduce the number of nuclear nations from 9 to 7 by making France and UK the only nations apart from Russia that are nuclear from Europe with no nuclear arsenals making Europe nuclear- disarmed which will help Russia launch its campaign against Europe/NATO.

## China:

China is still at a war, A civil war. See in 1949 a rebellion started in ROC - Republic of China and demanded a new nation called PRC- People's republic of China. The ROC also had mainland China and Taiwan in their control. But the PRC throwed away the ROC from the Mainland and claimed ROC theirs but they also wanted the island of Taiwan and so no peace treaty had been signed and so they are still officially in a civil war. But besides this fact, China has a strategy of Belt and Road initiative and dept trap. China indirectly invades nations by making a friendship with them. But how? China gives big loans, big loans amount? The big loan amounts are given by the Economy of the nation. China gives a loan big enough to contribute to the economy of the nation. Yeah, and not for the development, for the destruction. Becuase whatever is built by the money only Chinese companies should get the contract and they don't even tell them how to make it and the labor force is also Chinese. But if the country is not able to pay the loan China automatically gets the build for at least 100 years. But now the loans are so big given that the other country has no other option but to take more loans or give the build to China. Countries panic and use the money that is for development to pay loans and remember they are small countries so they don't even have enough money but then their money finishes, loan is left and they in hurry sell their land or give them the build.

There is a One belt, one road initiative with many mini-initiatives like belt and road project, string of pearls etc. to tackle the big countries like India, European nations and USA by building roads and ports sounds funny isn't it. So, the plan is that they started a project that main objective told to their countries was to improve road connectivity and yes this was one of the objectives becuase China is a trade hub. But the other hidden Goal was to trap big countries who are not supporting them. They made a web around big countries so that China can block them via land and Sea routes. But yet China and many other countries have more strategies that are not revealed becuase why should they do so?

One belt, One road

# *India:*

India has many tactics on how to fight two-way wars but some things are a secret! But like China has strings of pearl India has Necklace of diamonds initiative but to tackle China's influence and doesn't have dirty plans like China does. Indian force doesn't need much of strategies as they are expert in any terrain from Himalayan Mountain range to Forests, Plains and water. In the south there is water and India is very powerful in navy. Indian army is expert in forests and mountains and all this contributes to about 70% of India's borders. Now in plains fights are never too easy so we can't have an estimate but the countries near to India are most in the dept trap of China which is a big problem for India. But the army, navy and Airforce is too strong. India has taken the necklace of diamonds strategy really serious, acquired many ports in important strategic locations, completed projects, built roads and much more.

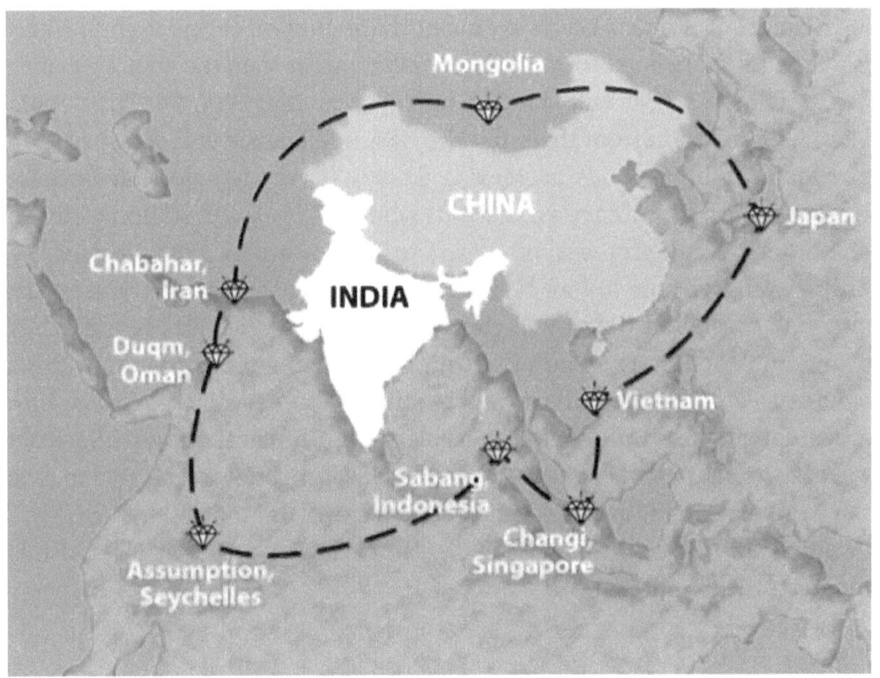


Necklace of Diamonds

## MAJOR ATTACK PLANOUTS:

*These are the major attacks some countries have in thier minds over some countires so that if you live in those countries you could plan out to move in the event of a World War 3. ( Its your choice)*

### *USA-*

USA could be attacked from 3 major fronts, and those are-
1. Mexico
2. East Coast
3. West Coast

Now let's dive into these. So first of all, the most least possible- The Mexican front. Mexico, I can't say about the alignment of this country like it is a little bit more bend towards the socialist rather than the west. If Mexico had to choose one, it will choose China rather than USA. So China could launch an invasion from there but the USA intelligence will detect as soon as China's military lands on Mexico So this is very less possible becuase USA will move its military and alert its whole military and station badly on all borders with heavy weapons ready to destroy attack from all sides. So, China would be able to fool USA. So they have only 2 options. West coast and east coast, and China will choose West coast. Why? Becuase Earth is round and becuase It is round so China is near the west coast. But China would need to hide the Soldiers very carefully. Also, very major cities of USA are situated here so USA needs to be alert. But China can attack USA from the east coast after the west coast so that USA army doesn't be able to save the east coast and if both are captured, I'm sure That 1/3 of USA's GDP will be gone. But they still would have the same military power as most of it is hidden it the mainland USA.

## *China:*

China can get attack from these Areas-
    1. Tibet
    2. Xinjiang
    3. Coastal Areas and Manchuria

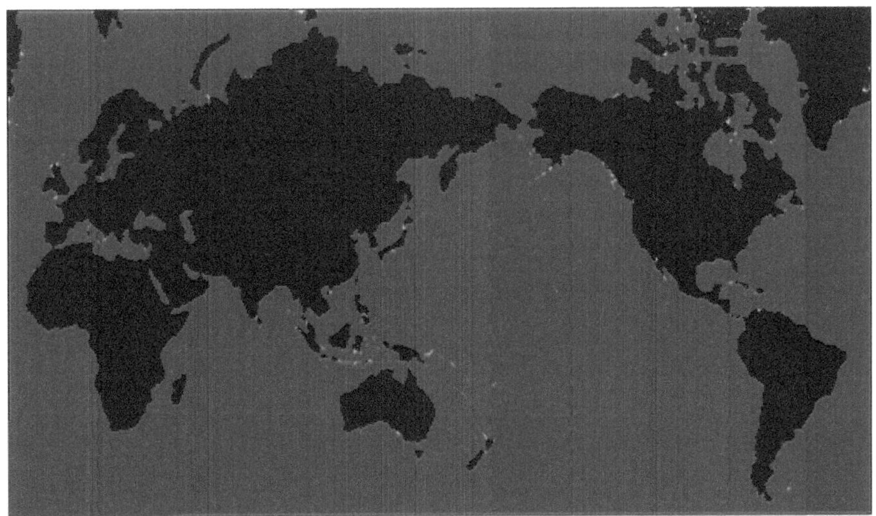

Tibet is going to be one of the hardest battle grounds for China as the war most probably is going to be with the USA aligned country and one of the biggest competitors of China, India. Thus, war is going to be hard for both and will be close, China has advantage in tech but India can easily defeat China in the mountain range on which China shares a border with India. India is also developing in tech so this is going to really close and especially becuase India has the support of USA.

So, it is most probably going to be a loss for China. But China would like to recover and that is going to be by The Xinjiang front where they can easily wipe out the countries easily and so now let's move on to the hardest front for China, Coast and Manchuria province of China. Here they will have to defeat South Korea, Japan, Taiwan and USA and you know USA, Japan and South Korea in top ten most powerful ones and we have to remember that their military is distributed in a lost fight with India and Xinxiang province bordering countries so this is also going to be a lost fight.

So we can safely say that China has lost becuase India will also block their 80% trade by blocking the Malacca strait and then they will be bankrupt. Didn't got a map of it.

## *Russia:*

Apologies to Russia, but the scenario suggests a significant territorial loss. The country is likely to face pressure on multiple fronts, with Europe and NATO advancing from the west, while the USA could target the Siberian region. However, it is possible that inner Russia may remain intact, as both the USA and NATO might not push too deeply into Russian territory. Despite this, it is anticipated that Russia will no longer be the largest country in the world. That being said, I want to clarify that I am not predicting outcomes; I aim to keep this book grounded in factual analysis, so I will refrain from delving further into speculative scenarios.

## *India:*

India is also at a hard stance so these are the fronts India is going to face-
1. Himalyan Front
2. Kashmiri Front

To simplify, Himalayan front borders Tibetan front so you can consider them a bunch of mountains that two countries divided and ruled and no I'm not talking about the divide and Rule policy. Kashmir is another mountain range near to the both of them but with a different name. So, in both of these fronts India is going to face two big powers China and Pakistan both very strong, but Pakistan lacks a lot in different things and they are barely in the top 10 as their military rank fall this year! How shocking! So, it will not be surprising that Pakistan will be out of the top ten military powers by 2025 becuase their military is busy in controlling their country and painting their houses that they most of the time forget to defend their borders. They don't let any government even finish their 5 years term and do a military coup so in war they will have two things, control their nation and war and they get more profit in controlling the nation so they will most probably give up land and control their nation! Simple. But I'm not here to explain Pakistan's internal politics becuase I do not belong from there so I don't know much about there. So, we have already talked about the war in the Chinese side and how there could be a stalemate or India will win. So, this is for this Chapter.

# FOUR

## MODERN TYPES OF WARFARE

Modern types of Warfare have come. I talked about the general fashion way of warfare in detail. Now I will talk about the new types, modern types of warfare's which are becoming more and more relevant day by day, although I'll not talk much about it, but I will talk about it in this chapter, these will definitely be used in World War 3:

1. Cyber Warfare
2. Guerrilla warfare
3. Terrorism
4. Resource Warfare
5. Diplomatic Warfare
6. Ideological Warfare

### 1.Cyber Warfare:

As you know, this is the technology era, so internet rules the world, and we would suffer a recession, not a big one, but a significant one. Each second of internet stopped in the entire world is billions of dollars lost. So, Countries use this type of warfare, to hijack the internet of the opposing country, leave them stunned, and when internet is not available, soldiers' loose connection, people panic, economy suffers government is disconnected from the country, and the other side gets the chance to advance into the other country with only a slight bit of resistance.

## 2.Guerrilla Warfare:

Guerrilla warfare is meant to disrupt military operations and irritate the country by independent forces mostly funded by other nations that are at war with the other nations so that they can get a highly easy time to invade till the forces again reach the border. This is very dangerous for the common public too. In Guerilla warfare they try to surprise enemy in such a way that they get distracted and their forces get split into the new front to deal with this. This is mainly used in stalemates and in this situation enemy nation uses gorilla warfare to push back/ push forwards the other country.

## 3.Terrorism:

Facing Terrorism is a very hard task for any country. It tries to divide the country into two separate parts because of the following reasons: -

1. **External funding:** from a less powerful nation which cannot face the power of the other nation.
2. **Internal Uprising:** If it is an internal uprising, It is the nation's government's problem which they rename as Terrorism to get out of trouble.
3. **Migration:** Sometimes heavily migrated groups from other nations are not treated well/ are not well-mannered start terrorist activities for employment.

**Whatever the reason be, we must not let terrorist do anything, because they harm infra, public, and the deprive the reputation and value of the land.** Also, we can learn how to deal with terrorist by **India** as they have retaliated to terrorist that their reputation is declining rapidly and they are at their last stages and are trying to be existent. The terrorist hub, Kashmir is now anti- terrorist. Terrorist now attack common public rather than soldiers that means their moral has been rapidly killed brutally.

## 4.Resource Warfare:

Resources are depleting quickly. Countries hate to import but like to export. But if they don't have resources, they have no other choice but to simply import it which they don't really like. So countries fight to get essential resources like **oil. If they don't get it on their own soil, they make allies which will provide them those resources on cheap prices.** So, they fight on which ally they can get.

## *Water:*

For this topic, we need to understand how do maritime borders of a country work, you can see the image below for further reference to the topic. So, the maritime sea borders of a country are divided into 3 parts, Territorial Sea, contiguous zone, and EEZ (Exclusive Economic Zone).

1.Now, the Territorial Sea totally belongs to the country and they can have any laws implemented there, Airspace above it is also their and they control the whole area and do whatever they want. The zone starts from the baseline to 12 miles of the sea.

2. Then, the contiguous zone starts from 12 miles of the sea to 24 miles of the sea. In this zone you don't have control over the Airspace of the zones but still all the control of the water in the zone.

3. Then, EEZ (Exclusive Economic Zone) begins from 24 miles to 200 miles of the sea body in which you only have the control of the resources found in the sea and you can only experiment in that sea area.

In the 21' century countries want resources and ocean has high number of resources so countries want maximum EEZ to own those resources legally. According to international law, you can increase your EEZ by submitting a request in the UN and if your report is reasonable and the EEZ you want to expand into is not already claimed by some other country you will b given a permit to take that EEZ for yourself. Countries are rushing to get most of the EEZ but nearby countries mostly have overlapping claims and requests get reject. To this date, only 9 countries have been able to expand their EEZ and 100 have submitted requests which haven't been accepted yet. UN also suggests 30 nations to expand their EEZ which have not submitted yet.

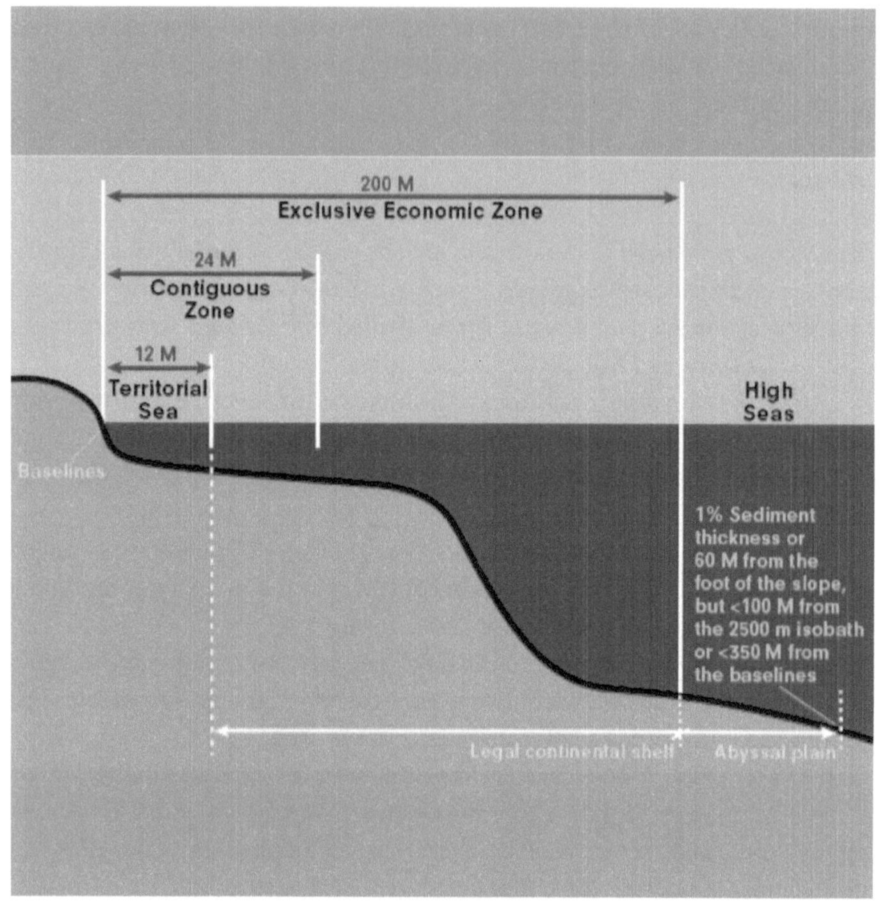


## 5.Diplomatic Warfare:

Diplomatic warfare relies on alliances formed based on strategic significance rather than ideology. Generally, there are three primary sides: the superpower, the opponent, and the neutral nations. As discussed in previous chapters, the USA represents the superpower, Russia stands as the opponent, and the remaining countries fall into the neutral category. The USA, with its long history, has established strong connections with other nations, while Russia, having gained independence in a weakened state in 1991, has managed to remain resilient. Russia is now striving to build alliances with neutral nations and strengthen its relations with other global powers. In this geopolitical landscape, every nation, no matter how small, plays a role in the broader diplomatic game.

## 6. Ideological Warfare:

This warfare is not to be used in World War 3 and was never used in any of the world wars. This is just for your common knowledge. This war is fought on Ideologies, Whose system works best, is the best. This almost caused a world war nowadays known as cold war. Although the war didn't started, because Communism's core, Soviet Union collapsed before in 1991.

# FIVE
# THE GLOBAL IMPACT

Now, lets talk about consequences. As I told you, Catastrophic consequences we will face. Let's make it easy to understand. World War 3 will have multiple consequences, some slightly bad, some Catastrophic. So, I will divide these consequences into 8 categories- Shocking but fascinating right! Also note, if the $3^{rd}$ Impact takes place, then all of the other impacts will not be practical. But if $3^{rd}$ Impact doesn't take pace, then all other impacts will take place as environment in the controller of this war-

    *1.Geopolitical Impact*
    *2.Economic Impact*
    *3.Industrial Impact*
    *4. Environmental Impact*
    *5. Humanitarian Impact*
    *6.Metal and Cultural Impact*
    *7.Govermental Impact*
    *8.Technological Impact*

---

We will discuss about all of them. You read one Impact per day as I also know it is too big to read as once.

## *1.Geopolitical Impact*

The most Important point is this. Geopolitical Impact, for which this World War will start also. This is simple, borders will shift, dynamics will change, puppet states will change, maybe capitalism, the current ideology of the world, can lose power or can become more influential on the world stage. Puppet states will get created, new kingmakers will emerge, Superpower will definitely shift, maybe it can be a USA ally or enemy. Borders will change, some will gain, while some left with loss. Next part of this book will simulate this part of this war.

## 2. *Economic Impact*

Economic Impact of this war will be heavy on this world. Let's divide this into three Impacts-

1. Reconstruction Cost
2. Recession
3. Global Trade

- **Reconstruction Cost** will be high and heavy for the governments of all countries that survive to see the aftermath of this war. The new land gained with be totally destroyed and places where wars where at a stalemate for a long time would require lot of money to reconstruct. Economy would not be able to sustain this growth, so a lot of money would be taken and would put pressure on the economy at its neck and if the pressure is to much the economy will collapse and then a depression period will start.
- **Recession** occurs when there is a period of reduced output and significant increase in unemployment rate. World War 3 is a disastrous event and companies will collapse so they're will be a period of reduced output and as a result, massive unemployment. The economy suffers bad in this period as inflation spikes and it is very hard to pull out a country of this situation especially after fighting a World War and only a few powerful countries stay with a stable economy.
- **Global Trade** will be damaged as countries will choke others trade and countries who imported the materials and who exported, both will be in lose.

## *3. Technological and Industrial Impact*

Because of World War 3, industries will focus on making weapons and hence production of other things will be less while not at its ending stage. This will affect industries and markets for the next 2-3 decades heavily. If serious actions are not taken against this weapon industry after the war, weapons are going to be produced in mass after the war also, as the factories made by the owners cannot just be closed after millions of dollars of investment. Yeah, these industries will come to an end eventually as the overflow of weapons increase in the market and needs are met completely for the next 100 years. This will be on a mass scale in the small countries if they survive in this war as during the war, they will the most to open such factories to even fight the war and try to survive. Big countries have much tighter law (Except USA but they have power) which will make it easier to eradicate the problem in a shorter time period. Also, new military weapons will be created during that war, so we will see a new wave of weapons in the market, like it happened in World War 2 when Nukes were invented and now, they rule the weapon industry and are considered a power scale of a country and every country wants it. We will see a similar wave after World War 3.

## 4.Environmental Impact

This is the point where the world will regret to start World War 3. The infrastructure, which human beings made putting lots of money, manpower, and effort will be in shambles. World will be a place where fallen buildings will be spread everywhere. Walking a step would be hard, no hospitals, religious buildings, malls or parks. It will be like the situation when an asteroid struck earth and dinosaurs vanished. The only difference would be that they're would be cement with fire and fire will not be alone. Nuclear fallout will make human sculptures spread everywhere s we saw with the dinosaurs. Quadrillions wasted. Earths resources drained and extinction of Humans, this is what geniuses say. Also, Trees support life on this planet. But, not even a single tree will survive near the radius of 100 kilometers of the nuclear bomb drop and this will make the re-evaluation of the land even worse.

## 5.Humanitarian Impact

They're will be a huge amount of displacement of people moving from here to there, for a safe place and the safe places like Switzerland, New Zealand will get flooded and a refugee crisis will be there with millions unfortunately left dead. Health Crisis will be in place as hospitals will lose safety because nowadays when wars are not on a big scale, all the wars have at least 1- 2 hospitals shot down. Nuclear radiation, massive flood of patients, less infra to manage patients and hospitals at risk will be the main cause of this health crisis. Many human rights will be broken but this is not the area I have a knowledge in.

## 6.Mental and Cultural Impact

Due to this war, many old heritage sites will be destroyed, cultures will be redesigned, due to the war major cultural events will be hard to conduct and hence the cultural reinforcement in countries which is at a declining level will be rapidly declining in countries and so many cultures will be changed from what they were. Survivors of the war will suffer badly from mental trauma for multiple years which could change their life outlook and lifestyle completely.

## 7.Governance Impact

UN, the current peacekeeping body will be questioned on their peacekeeping stances on this world and why they could stop this World War 3. Governing models will be changed according to the war outcome to being more democratic or Authoritarian. An Authoritarian regime has a concentration of power in a leader or in an elite not constitutionally responsible to the people.

## 8.Technological Impact

The last but not the least of the impacts, Tech online, cyberwarfare is going to be used in this war to disrupt the markets and online country systems so that the whole country's internet could be disrupted and they could move further into the war into a winning stance. I have explained this part in the previous parts of this book.

These are going to be the impacts of World War 3, while summarized in a short chapter, its real-life application is going to be big and devastating.

# SIX

# "THE ULTIMATE PEACEKEEPER"

## <u>UN</u>

### *United nations History and current*

In 1920's, when the 1st World War ended in heavy destruction of Europe when Europe was already controlling 70% of the world and one more war could steal all the world dominance they gained and their reputation could fall, they didn't want a war. So, the USA created a organization, League of Nations which tried to stop another World War and save Europe as the USA was rapidly developing on the basis Europe was importing from them weapons, and Europe was running on how much they get help in the redevelopment of their cities by the USA.

So, this organization was formed. But the 2nd world war happened with more destruction than ever and complete devastation of Europe. Then Disaster strikes, as I said before, one war could destroy their dominance over the world and so it started. One After another, people protest for freedom, Europe weak from the war cannot fight so gives independence. And so, the cycle continues and Europe lost the World, Literally.

But A new peace organization was formed to maintain world peace, this time seriously. From deploying forces to hosting important decisions, not for one's benefits, but for all. It wasn't made to maintain someone's world order, it was made to maintain peace. It was a platform to find solutions, solve conflicts and it did. For the past 74 years, it stopped a world war. But everything finds a bias in it and so did United Nations. It is not that old UN as before. It cannot stop wars, cannot tackle modern warfare and is stick to stop only the old, Second World war tactics. Nowadays wars are fought different from before, from tech and not only me, many people have the sentiment UN is going to fail in stopping World War 3. Little number of resolutions are passed. New world powers are not welcomed in the security council and a single bill "Is Islamophobia a threat" is asked again and again and the answer is always no. No talks on other religions and war related resolutions are not two sided. Although countries from various parts of world are trying to bring reforms in UN. So lets see where it goes. UN was a peacekeeper, Is a peacekeeper, but cannot continue this honor in the future without reforms.

# SEVEN

## INTERESTING MICRO-TOPICS!

This is the index part of this chapter for your navigation, chose what you want to read and enjoy! -

1. Nuclear Aspect
2. NATO
3. Protests and people
4. Technology
5. Aftermath of the war
6. Impact on You
7. Geographical Impact
8. Sanctions

**1. Nuclear Aspect**

Hiroshima and Nagasaki Nuclear bomb drop

Nuclear Aspect is the most devastating. The nuclear bomb dropped on Hiroshima and Nagasaki on Japan, 1945 to end World War 2 was devastating as you know. Both cities have recovered and thrive today but the bomb killed 210,000 people at that time. It has been 77 years since the bomb was dropped and nuclear tech has advanced more and more. If the bomb was so disastrous then, So, after 77 years how powerful it might be and so I present you a research paragraph for the comparison.

- Weight of the Little Boy (nuclear bomb dropped by United States of America)- 4,400 kg
- Weight of a tsar bomba (Best nuclear bomb) – 27,000 kg

**Destruction parameter of Little boy bomb if it hit UK-**

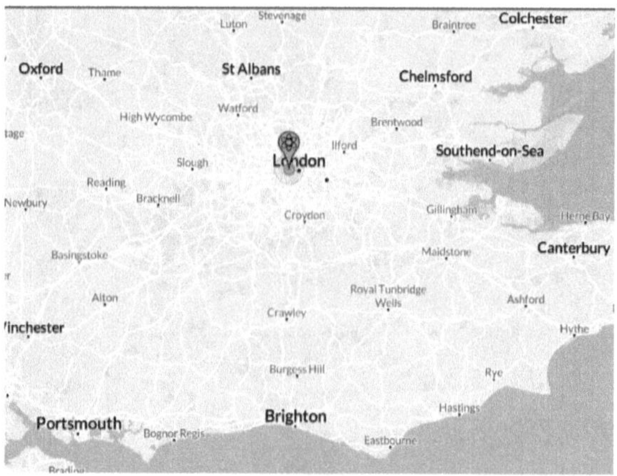

Little boy Impact zone

**Destruction parameter of Tsar bomba if it hit UK-**

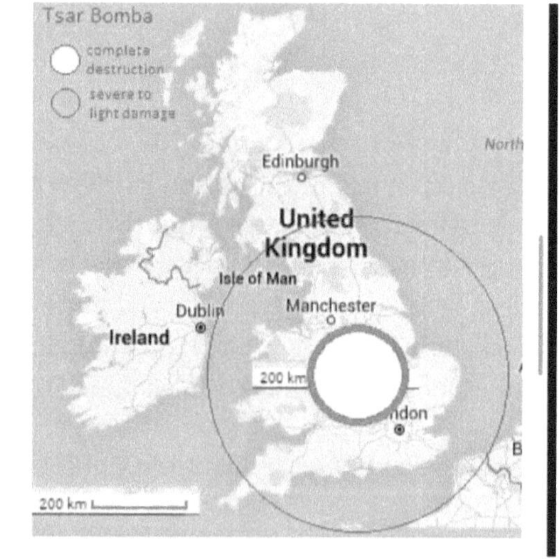


Tsar bomba impact zone

So, this is the end of this comparison. Now, lets talk in general. A mushroom cloud will cover the infected area. A whole generation will get multiple diseases and most common will be the mighty deadly cancer. A nuclear bomb can infect a whole continent with a plaque of acid. Acid Rains will be a big spreader of this plaque and air will transport this to a whole continent. A big example of this is the Chernobyl nuclear plant disaster. While nuclear plants and nuclear bombs are of different use, they use the same power, nuclear energy. Whether the energy is used for good or wars the energy has the same power. So, lets get back to the topic. Chernobyl nuclear disaster in short was a leakage of nuclear toxic energy which plagued the entire continent of Europe from Ukraine (Where the disaster happened under USSR) to UK. Acids rains happened all over the continent of Europe. The Area of the past Chernobyl nuclear plant in still unhabitable and deadly to go to. All people in the surrounding area of the plant were killed and Europe soon after reduced the number of nuclear plants. Now these affects will still be applicable when a nuclear bomb in by chance exploded. Micro topic 1 concludes here.

## 2. NATO

-NATO is one of the most well-known alliances today, known by the whole world as a strong alliance with 32 countries which include a strong powerhouse of USA, UK, Germany, Poland, France, Italy, Greece and Turkey which have a very big military and 24 small countries relying on NATO protection from Russia but still contribute a large number of soldiers. This Alliance was made to stop soviet expansion to the western parts of Europe and now serves as a protective alliance from Russia which is believed to be the successor state of USSR.

-This alliance has 3.42 million active-duty soldiers and 3 million reserves too which is double or sometimes triple from the Russian Military. NATO includes Nuclear Armed States and has a mega economy to support a World War.

-Therefore, NATO countries are not taken for granted and any war waged on NATO will lead us a step not closer this time but into the war!

## 3.Protests and People

This War will lead to protests all over the world to stop the world and people will terrorist ambitions will attack the country when the country is at its weakest point, a point where half the military in somewhere else fighting for their so-called Allies and rest fighting wars with their hostile neighbors. Terrorists will capture many areas, many new countries will be formed along, and neighbors will infiltrate and capture the country in this weak point as soon as possible. Terrorist groups will be at their peak and will grow at a frightening rate. Whole governments could fall and the world could be totally different. Every nation will have to fight a three-front war, whether its neighbors or terrorists. Many billionaires will fund a side which will benefit their business survival and personal interests.

## 4. Technology

The tech industry, will be facing a mix of advancement and destruction because of the War. During the time period of the war, new technology will be introduced in the military aspect of Tech. Such tech and we would have not ever imaged too. Vehicles on supersonic speeds or aircrafts near the speed of light. Military innovation would be the must for scientists to survive and profit the war led society. But on the flip side on the coin, tech will suffer too as many scientists making revolutionary tech will be forced to focus on Military tech inventions and some of the most secret tech blueprints could be destroyed too such as Semiconductors which are a must need product in the present. If we compare this to the present situation, the positives are above negatives but in a situation of World War, Positives and Negatives will be equal leading to maximum tech innovation in some fields but less in others, Leading to a situation of disbalance.

## 5. Aftermath of the War

So, now let's talk about the Aftermath of this war, which is seriously a little scary to think of! So, many independent states will form, some will expand, some will decrease, some will not exist and others will be neutralized. SO, this will general but now let's talk in the internal terms. Terrorists group will gain power, control over the political world and reach their agenda's easily of breaking nations apart and forming own governments. The world would be in a very dangerous state of terrorists. Almost every nation with an active terror group will be at 50/50 stakes of falling and not falling. A world controlled by terror will establish in case of a heavy world war put into place. Military forces will have a hard time in establishing state of order in the countries and some small military nations might fall to terrorists for a long time. Some big nations might also fall to terrorists facing hard time in controlling more than half of its territory to this date and a big example is Pakistan. Internal stability will be at its lowest point and the winning side might also lose themselves internally to terror or public opinion. In conclusion, half of the countries might not be as similar as they are today. Nuclear Aftermath is already covered in the upper part of this chapter.

## 6. Impact on You

Impact on you, is a section where I introduce the effects of the war on you, your money, your value and your daily life! First of all, there are very less chances of people surviving in an atomic World War 3. But incase this war is only limited till conventional warfare, the effect on you will be huge.

First of all, inflation will be in double digits and triple digits applicable for almost all countries involved. For those who don't know about inflation, inflation is the rate of devaluation of your money. Like what costs 1$ back 100 years might be now 1000$ so the value of your money decreases in simple terms. Recession will plaque the world and almost all countries will be out of funds. That means they're will be a sharp cut or removal of subsidies and initiatives which benefits you daily.

Not only your pocket will be affected, but health too. Mental health will be in shambles, but physical health will be finished too. It will be too unsafe to go outside as any missile could strike your area during a time of total war and so health will be at danger. Hospitals will be not safe too, as the understanding of not targeting hospitals is being slowly demolished and we can see this happen in today's world where in both the war currently escalating have got a shot on 1 hospital at least. We that said, your daily life will be at danger too as businesses will close, companies will be not functional or shot by the enemy for war reasons, you will not get money to survive. Yes, Companies that work online will survive but rest will be demolished. Companies will face major losses as their stocks get destroyed and thousands of crores of products are wasted.

## 7. Geographical Impact

This is not about countries, which is geopolitics. But this is about terrain, in simple terms land. They're will be huge craters on the places where there were once plains while places with uneven terrain will be flattened and for people not still thinking it to be deadly, I must simply say, your houses, buildings and all things made by humans above ground will be flattened too and that too not in a good manner. This flattened land will be unhabitable struck by missiles several times will make hundreds of chemicals to release on the impacted area and make it unhabitable and areas covered with mushroom clouds will be deadly to even walk in. Mushroom cloud is an effect created when too much atomic energy explodes. Different vibrant terrain features maybe harmed and different unique nature magical places can be harmed too. We should try our best to protect these places and force countries to save our planets.

## 8. Sanctions

Sanctions are a contentious issue, often viewed as both a necessary measure and a harsh imposition. From one perspective, they are seen as a means to compel countries to cease harmful activities; from another, they are criticized for disproportionately affecting ordinary citizens who bear the brunt of the economic hardships, despite having no role in their government's actions. Sanctions typically involve restrictions imposed by one country on another, targeting various aspects such as imports, exports, military equipment, or access to certain systems, with the intent to pressure the sanctioned government.

However, while sanctions are designed to weaken the targeted country, they can have the opposite effect in the long run. The sanctioned nation may discover its true allies, become more self-reliant, and reduce its dependence on foreign goods and services. Historically, many sanctions have failed to achieve their intended goals, instead strengthening the resilience of the sanctioned country over time. In my view, sanctions should be used cautiously, as they often end up empowering the very nations they aim to weaken.

# EIGHT

## GEOPOLICTICAL FUN FACTS

1.There is an imaginary circle in south east Asia (Valerie Pieris Circle) which consists of 4.2 billion people! And the shocking fact is that it covers only 10% of the land area of earth. So more than half of the world population lives in a circle only covering 10% of land area

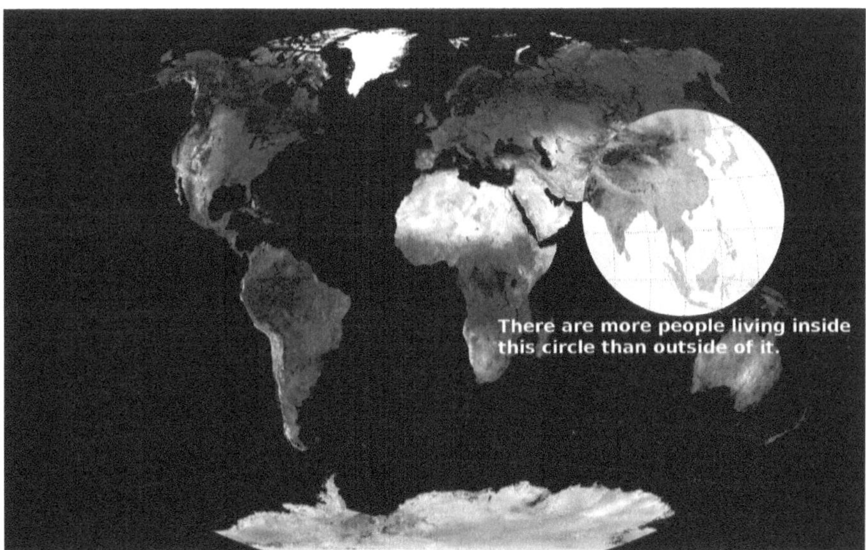


2.World is divided into two hemispheres as you know, Eastern and western hemisphere. The middle of these hemispheres is said to be

Greenwich, UK. Now, if you move east from Greenwich, you will gain 4 minutes every degree you move and if you move west from Greenwich, you will lose 4 minutes every degree. So, every 14 degrees you move, you will gain or lose 1 hour. Every country chooses 1-12 degrees of lines to be the time zone of a particular area. Some countries chose only one degree as their time zone. So, this map tells us everything in a more detailed and pictured form.

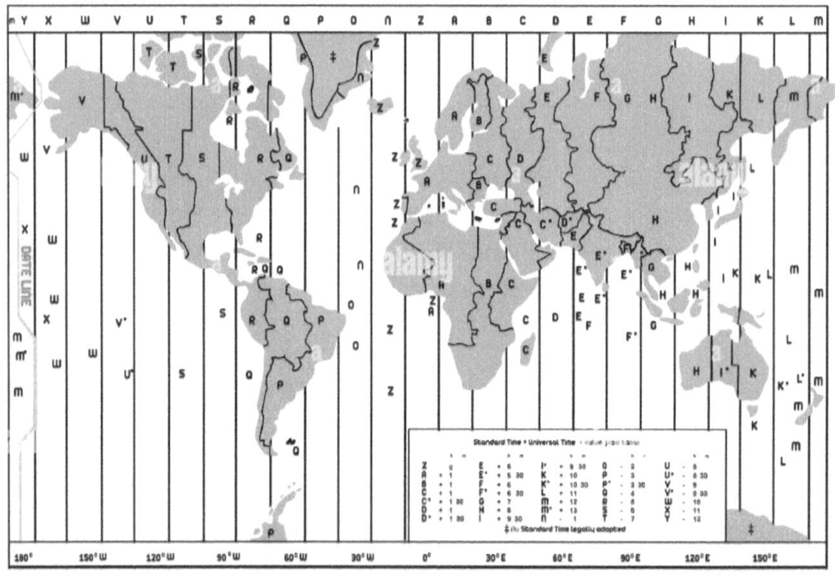


**3.** Did you know that if Britain never lost any of their colonies, what would they look like-

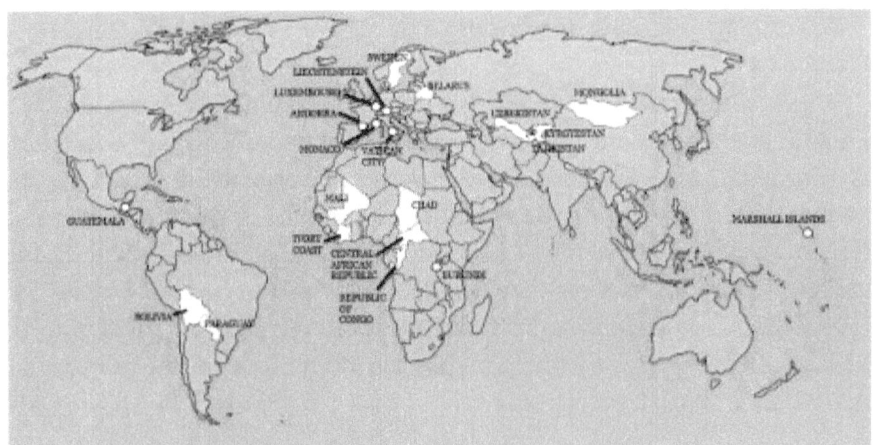


All countries Britain ever attacked

Same thing if applied to France-

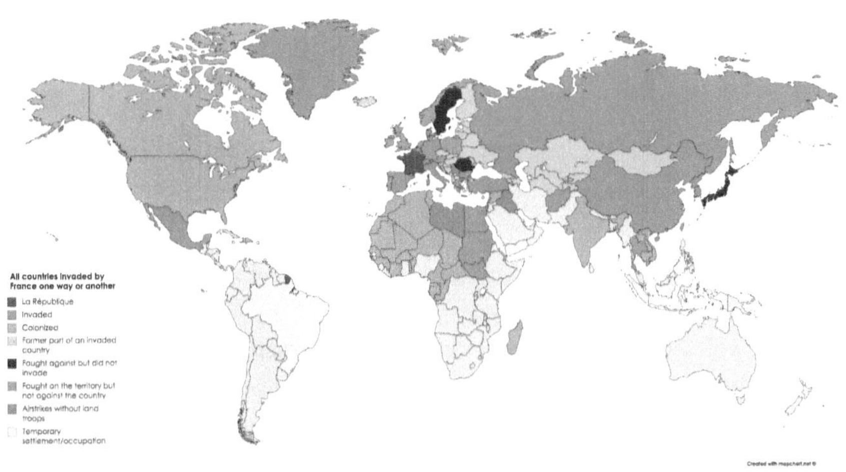


Lands ever touched by France

**4.** The World map that we use today is known as the Mercator's prediction and the countries near to Equator are shown small in the Mercator's prediction and countries towards the poles are way to extracted. It spreads misinformation about countries real sizes and was originally made for shipping boats. One of the famous examples is Greenland being very small in comparison to Africa but shown same on the Mercator's Prediction.

**5**. Everyone knows that Russia is a very large country. However, did you know that the Russian Empire, the precursor to the Russian Federation, once owned Alaska? The empire was so vast and unstable that it sold Alaska to the United States to raise funds for its administration. The Russian Federation still regrets this decision, as Alaska has become a significant source of natural resources for the USA. This sale occurred because the Russian Empire was financially devastated after World War I. On March 30, 1867, the United States agreed to pay Russia $7.2 million for the territory of Alaska, equating to 2 cents per acre.

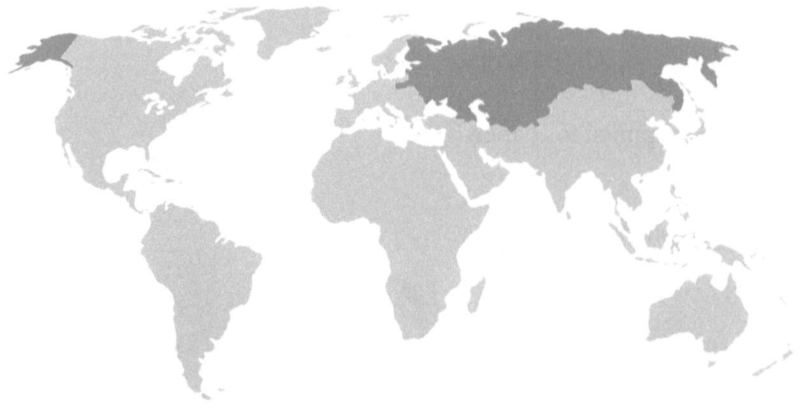

**Russian Empire at 1876 some days or months before Alaska purchase**

**6**. The collision between the Indian and Eurasian tectonic plates led to the formation of the Himalayan mountain range, which includes the highest mountain on Earth, Mount Everest. To elaborate, approximately 100 million years ago, a supercontinent called Pangea existed, with all landmasses connected. Over time, Pangea began to break apart into separate tectonic plates, leading to the formation of the world as we know it today.

The Indian tectonic plate, initially part of this breakup, started moving rapidly towards the Eurasian plate and away from Madagascar. Eventually, it collided with the Eurasian plate. Due to the lower elevation of the Indian plate compared to the Eurasian plate, the Indian plate was forced underneath the Eurasian plate. This subduction caused the Eurasian plate to be pushed upwards, resulting in the formation of the Himalayas.

This tectonic activity is ongoing, and the height of the Himalayas continues to increase as the Indian plate keeps colliding with the Eurasian plate. This process is cyclic, contributing to the continuous growth of the majestic Himalayas, which are home to numerous rivers, diverse flora, fauna, and natural beauty.

**Formation of The Himalayas**

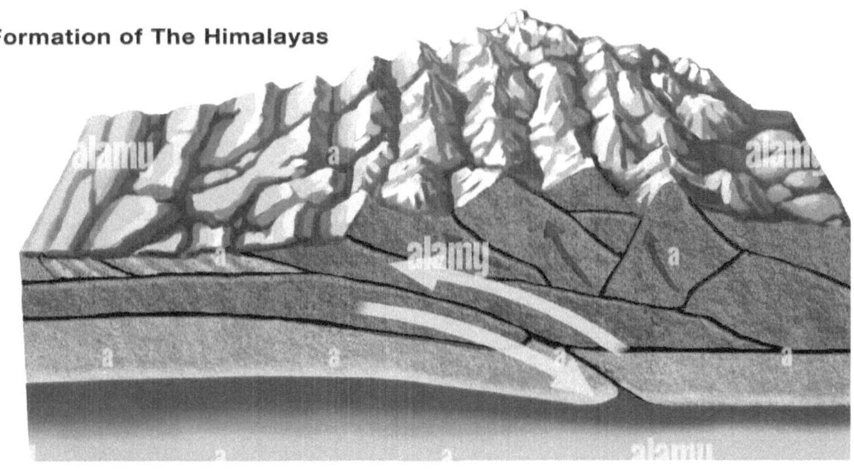

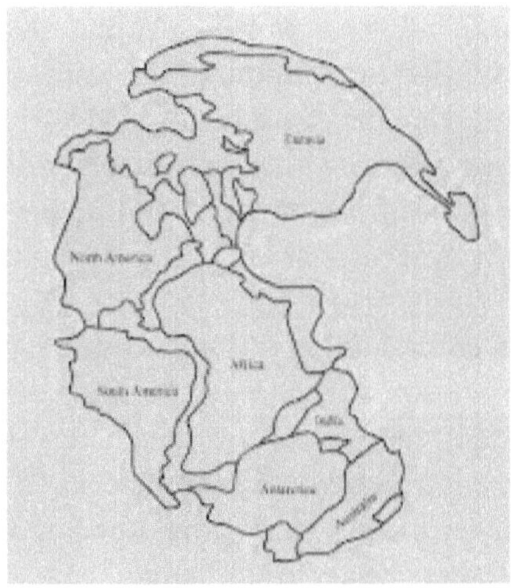

## Pangea

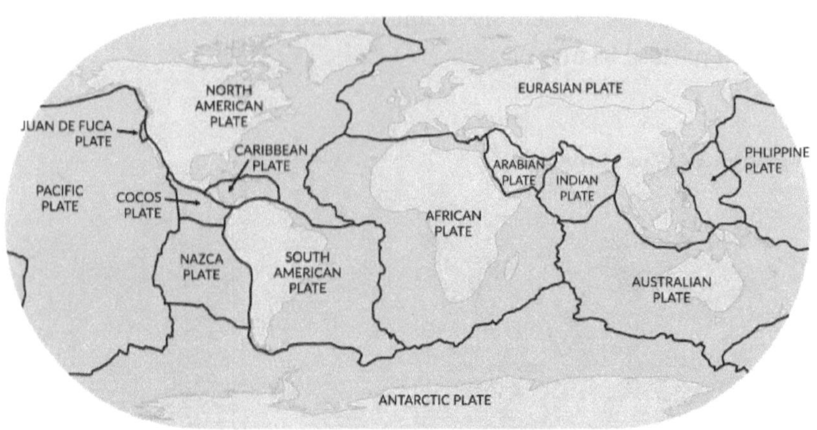


Tectonic Plates

**7.** Russia is considered the largest country on Earth. However, the strategic region of Kaliningrad Oblast often goes unnoticed. One might wonder why Russia possesses this isolated piece of land in the heart of Europe. The history dates back to the era of the USSR, when it wielded significant power and influence globally. During this time, Kaliningrad Oblast was part of the German Empire, which was later transformed into Nazi Germany under Hitler and engaged in World War II. As is well-known, Nazi Germany lost the war to the Allies, which included France, the UK, the USSR, China, and several smaller nations. The USSR, positioned to the east of Nazi Germany, advanced westward, capturing Kaliningrad Oblast and Berlin.

As a result of its substantial contributions during the war, the USSR was granted certain powers. It made Poland independent and incorporated Kaliningrad Oblast into its territory. Although the USSR gained several other advantages, this topic warrants separate discussion. When the USSR dissolved into 15 independent states, the Russian Federation retained Kaliningrad, rather than ceding it to Lithuania.

Kaliningrad continues to be of strategic importance to Russia, providing access to the Baltic Sea, which remains ice-free year-round. In the event of a conflict between Russia and NATO, this oblast could enable Russia to isolate the Baltic states from NATO protection, thereby gaining a strategic advantage.

**8.** Greenland, renowned for its cold climate and unique geographical location, has a misleading name and experiences a six-month day and night cycle. In this book, I will discuss this cycle in detail. The six-month day and night cycle in Greenland occurs due to the Earth's rotation and tilt. This phenomenon can be observed in numerous online videos. As implied by its name, Greenland experiences continuous daylight for six months during the summer and continuous darkness for six months during the winter. The Earth's tilt causes Greenland to either face the sun continuously or not at all for half of the year. This situation has several negative impacts, with disrupted sleep cycles being one of the most significant. Although it does not affect a large population, it still has a ripple effect on the lifestyle of Greenland's inhabitants.

**9.**The Western population crisis is now highly noticeable, especially in developed countries such as Japan, South Korea, and various European nations. This issue is widespread throughout the Western world. It is particularly prevalent in developed countries due to rising living standards and increased cost of living. Excluding the USA, most developed countries are currently facing this problem and will continue to do so in the future unless serious action is taken. The population replacement rate is said to be an average of 2.2 children per woman; if the rate falls below this, the population decreases. For instance, South Korea has reached a critically low rate of less than 0.8. This rapid decline makes it very challenging to raise the rate back to even 2.

Cultural factors in these countries do not emphasize having children, contributing to the population decline. According to the UN's latest report, the global population will start to decline in 2083, at a peak of 10.2 billion people. India, currently the most populous country, is projected to begin declining in 2062. Meanwhile, China, the second most populous country, has been experiencing a population decline since reaching its peak in 2022.

**10.** As history tells us, Europe was the center for both the world wars. But why? So, the story starts from the Age of European exploration about 500 years ago, in the 15$^{th}$ century. European started finding new lands, claimed it to be theirs and suppressed the local population and government by armed means. They started colonizing well-established regions, which were not at peace, and took advantage of that to establish their control over the region. Sometimes it was done by companies and then given to the government, which made the work way easier for them as they got small excuses like business to enter the country and eat it in the future. There was a time when Europeans controlled more than half of the world. From the 17$^{th}$ century, when the age of exploration ended, to the 19$^{th}$ century, Europe ruled most of the world, and with this came problems. European countries were very vast and super strong. So, when the rivalry ignited over who controls land, relations began to break. Also, countries in the heart of Europe like Poland, Germany, and many Balkan countries didn't get the chance to colonize, and this made them weaker than much of the rest of Europe.

While the strong nations were somewhere allied such as the UK, France, and the USSR, which got a chance to expand. This situation developed furthermore and caused two world wars, with millions of deaths. The country that started the war was Germany! Some sides also changed; some strong nations might be on the weak nation's side, but the aggressors or starters of both the world wars were Germany or Austria-Hungary!

The European colonization started to fall as the so-called strong European nations became weak by the world wars and couldn't hold their colonies. The British Empire, one of the biggest and one of the first European colonizers, fell in 1996 when Hong Kong gained independence. But, if they hadn't colonized big nations which started the independence movement or didn't engage in both the World Wars, maybe some part of their empire may have been saved. But this happened for good, as they looted countries and started massacres.

**11.**Unfortunately, A breakdown of countries is a real- case possibility in today's world. Developed countries in Europe are at verge of collapse. Immigration is flooding their countries with peoples of different nationalities. Most of the people who migrate unfortunately have bad habits due to bad conditions and what they have faced in their own past. Robbery is one the statistics that hike when migration is done at heavy level. These people migrate to developed countries with fewer laws and easier restrictions. UK and France are being flooded by this and are facing huge protests from these migrated communities. Germany is at overload as it is providing heavy aid to Ukraine, stopped by US from getting gas from Russia, and is facing heavy migration.

Due to these reasons, German economy is suffering. Some countries are made unstable by US for personal reasons, some are unstable by themselves and this is causing a huge collapse of countries in the world and also reducing US's spear of influence and democracy which it is destroying itself. World War 3 can leverage this to a huge extent. We have to stop sanctions and follow the path of world development. US, is expecting to destroy the country to re-establish it in its own way. But this effort mostly fails and a huge anti USA country is made. For example, Venezuela, which has lots of oil reserves was served with sanctions by the Freedom Land. Now, the country is totally with Russia and China and USA cannot improve its relations now with Venezuela.

Here they lost the largest oil reserve country. The next example is Iran, in which a democratic government was falling in the 1980's. Now, the USA had the option to interfere and save the nation, but they served the country with sanctions the the powerhouse went to Russia and China. Now we cannot stop the nations by falling to themselves but if we solve rest of the problems, this problem will be much suppressed and very less countries will convert into a failed state every year.

**12.** The breakdown of countries is a genuine possibility in today's world. Developed countries in Europe are on the verge of collapse, as immigration floods their borders with people of different nationalities. Unfortunately, many immigrants bring undesirable habits due to the poor conditions and hardships they have faced in their past. Robbery rates tend to increase significantly when migration occurs on a large scale. These immigrants often move to developed countries with fewer laws and more lenient restrictions. The UK and France are experiencing significant unrest from these immigrant communities. Germany is also overwhelmed, providing substantial aid to Ukraine, being restricted by the US from obtaining gas from Russia, and facing high levels of migration. Consequently, the German economy is suffering.

Some countries are destabilized by the US for personal reasons, while others become unstable on their own, leading to a significant global collapse and diminishing US influence and democracy. World War 3 could exacerbate this situation. It is imperative to cease sanctions and pursue global development. The US aims to dismantle countries to reconstruct them in its own image, but this effort often fails, resulting in strong anti-US sentiments. For example, Venezuela, rich in oil reserves, faced sanctions from the US and is now aligned with Russia and China, severing its ties with the US. Similarly, in the 1980s, Iran's democratic government was faltering. Instead of intervening to save the nation, the US imposed sanctions, leading Iran to align with Russia and China. While it may be challenging to prevent nations from collapsing on their own, addressing the broader issues could significantly reduce the number of countries becoming failed states each year.

# A Personal Note

Thank you for reading until the end. I hope you found the content insightful, interesting, and that it has inspired you to form a new habit. This book has been my dream project, and I appreciate your valuable purchase. I am grateful for the trust you placed in choosing my book among thousands of others available to you. I will continue to create such insightful works to contribute to the world of knowledge. My next books will be nuclear Devastation, and Airplanes part 2. I will countinue to put great efforts like this in my future books!